THE CARDINAL STRITCH STORY

SAMUEL CARDINAL STRITCH

MARIE CECILIA BUEHRLE

The Cardinal Stritch
Story

THE BRUCE PUBLISHING COMPANY • MILWAUKEE

NIHIL OBSTAT:

JOANNES A. SCHULIEN, S.T.D.
Censor librorum

IMPRIMATUR:

✠ GULIELMUS E. COUSINS
Archiepiscopus Milwauchiensis
May 4, 1959

To all those who have loved
His Eminence, Cardinal Stritch,
to every beneficiary of his abounding charity,
this story of his life is wholeheartedly dedicated.

FOREWORD

IN EMPHASIZING as the central point, the focus, of the life of Cardinal Stritch, his dedication to his priestly vocation, the writer of this book has without question seized upon the most important aspect of his character.

Samuel A. Stritch was a priest for forty-eight years and it can be said in all truth that his life was concentrated and wholly spent in the priesthood. When as a young man he felt the first stirrings of his priestly vocation, he began to reflect and meditate assiduously on the priesthood. Even in those early years he seemed to understand fully that in the Catholic Church there is only one High Priest, Christ Himself, and each individual priest is "another Christ." This expression was for him the definition of the priest; he was fond of recalling it and commenting upon it, with a wealth of doctrine and warmth of spirit, whenever he spoke to priests.

He was, of course, well aware of the logical conclusion that flows from these words: if the priest is "another Christ" — *alter Christus* — he must then continue the work of Christ in extending the Church. This thought was a source of inspiration to him, and he liked to emphasize and illustrate in many ways that the Church rests on Christ Himself, as its foundation stone; He is the invisible Head, the Master, the Author of the Sacraments, and Fount of every grace. Peter is the visible rock or foundation and the visible head of the Church, and under the guidance of Peter and his successors, bishops and priests continue to work in the spirit of Christ's own *aedificabo* — "upon this rock I will build My Church" (Mt. 16:18).

They preach the Gospel and sanctify souls; in suchwise grace is poured forth in the hearts of men and the Church continues to be in very truth the *aedificatio Christi* — the building-up of Christ in souls and in the world. These thoughts furnished the food of meditation for the young Samuel Stritch. "Priesthood and Church" was the substance of his studies. From it he drew inspiration for his interior life.

In the Providence of God, his advantages were many. He always considered it a great privilege to have been able to complete his studies at the North American College in Rome, the center of Christianity, near the Chair of truth. In Rome, his love for the priesthood and the Vicar of Christ grew stronger and deeper and his already firm determination to dedicate himself to Christ and to the Church became even more pronounced.

This sense of dedication flowered into real ardor when he was ordained a priest at a very young age and began his ministry in his native Nashville. For eleven years he was an assiduous and untiring worker in the vineyard of the Lord. Then he was made Bishop when he was only thirty-four, and thus had both opportunity and position to enlarge and increase his cherished program of "Priesthood and Church": in Toledo for nine years, in Milwaukee for another nine years, and in Chicago from 1940 to his death.

A Good Shepherd, in the sense of our Lord's own parable, he "built" Christ in the souls of men by every possible means. Above all, he "built" by his own good example. Throughout his life he sought to give such example and his many friends were always edified (only another way of saying "built") by him. He was a model priest.

He thought of this, and his conscience rendered testimony to him, when shortly after his arrival in Rome he was obliged to leave the Collegio Santa Maria del Lago for the hospital where he later died. He knew that he was near his end, and to the priests who affectionately surrounded him he said: "I have always tried to be a good priest." Cicero's words were verified in him: "The consciousness of a well-spent life and the memory of many good deeds is most gratifying" (*De Senectute*, III, 9).

He was ever zealous, industrious, in preaching the word of truth. Rarely would he pass by the opportunity to remind his hearers of their Christian duties. He could well say, in the words of St. Paul:

"My dear children, with whom I am in labor again until Christ be formed in you" (Gal. 4:9).

But it was his particular joy to preach on the priesthood. His ideas and thoughts were substantially as follows: "The priest may never claim any credit to himself in his ministry because everything comes to him from our Lord; he dispenses the things of God, not his own; he preaches not his own word, but the doctrine of Christ; he administers the Sacraments which Jesus Christ has instituted; he is an ambassador and is strictly bound to fulfill his duties as a representative. He cannot even boast of his priestly vocation as something depending on or derived from his own personal choice and decision because he has been called by another."

And on the occasion of a priestly jubilee, he spoke as follows: "It is not that the fruit of the priest is his own, because his words are the words of Christ, and his ministry is the ministry of Christ; and still in a sense, as our blessed Saviour says, we may speak of the fruits of an individual priest. When that priest lovingly labors and works for the Saviour and unites himself in everything with our blessed Saviour, there come to him great graces and blessings, and he may even say that the souls he sanctifies and saves through Christ Jesus our Lord are his souls. Christ's works are his works. To understand this paradox we must be mindful that fidelity to Christ in the sacred Priesthood gives the priest a very share in the work which Christ does through him."

Speaking on another occasion, to encourage and stimulate his beloved priests, he said: "Look into the life of a Catholic people and you will see the fruits of the priest, see the sanctity, see the nobility, see the heroism in souls whose inspiration came from a priest. . . . The fullness of the fruits of a priest can never be recorded by man. Only God's recording angel holds the record of them. And so, if we do speak of a priest and the fruits of his work, at most we are only telling a part of the story. Still, it is good to tell what we see and what we know for our own edification and to bring souls to understand how much the priest has given them."

In addition, Cardinal Stritch "edified" — built, materially speaking. It would be difficult indeed to enumerate all the churches, the schools, the charitable institutions in Toledo, Milwaukee, and Chicago that owe their origin to his inspiration. He was deeply concerned about fostering in every way an intense parochial life. With the burning zeal of an apostle, he insisted upon the truth that the parish is the living organism by means of which the faith is spread in the family and in the community. It is the place, the means, offered by divine Providence to the faithful for their spiritual growth and perfection. And of the faithful who seek to live this parochial life one may say, in the words of St. Paul: "You are God's tillage, God's building" (1 Cor. 3:9).

Cardinal Stritch was fond of recalling the three beautiful cathedrals which were his. In building the cathedral in Toledo, he did so in a truly majestic fashion. These fine churches reminded him of the thousands of priests and countless faithful, who were confided to his care, who gathered with him to assist at solemn ceremonies, or submit to his attention new plans for various charitable endeavors. He rejoiced ever in the sight and the memory of these beautiful temples.

But one edifice in particular gave him special pleasure and that was the Retreat House for the Clergy on the grounds of St. Mary of the Lake Seminary in Mundelein, Illinois. He was happy that this specifically ecclesiastical foundation was the pride of his clergy.

Nature and grace were generous indeed to him, and they helped to make him a leader, and a great leader. He was such, too, as an American, proud of his great country, always eager to do his best to enrich it with spiritual treasures and charitable and educational institutes, inspiring others, both priests and people, to imitate him.

He was a great leader above all as a priest, truly a *sacerdos magnus* — a great high priest. He had a brilliant mind, a mild and even disposition; he was fond of study and reflection; he was humble, patient, pious. In the Sacred Heart of Jesus he found the inspiration to follow his Master; he followed Him with the cross and gave shining example of this in his last days on this earth.

Naturally, he was surprised and somewhat dismayed when the

invitation arrived from our late Holy Father, Pope Pius XII, of holy memory, to assume the high office of Pro-Prefect of the Sacred Congregation for the Propagation of the Faith. For a moment he felt rather lost, but then in prayer and reflection he regained his usual serenity. His attachment to his archdiocese of Chicago, its clergy and faithful, was strong and deep. His whole life was wrapped up in the diocese, one of the largest and most flourishing in the world.

Finally, when it became necessary for the Holy See to receive a reply and prepare a statement for publication, I was so informed and I telephoned to His Eminence. My question was simple and brief: "Do you accept?" He replied: "It is the Holy Father who calls me."

We continued to talk and the Cardinal stressed in the conversation that a bishop must give his priests good example of obedience. The sacrifice involved in leaving his archdiocese and country would be rewarded by the honor conferred on the United States. Then too, he was attracted by his love for Rome which he always thought of as his second home and by the opportunity thus offered to advance the cause of the Missions throughout the world. He accepted the call, both as a sacrifice and as a joy.

He had scarcely arrived in Rome when he passed to his eternal reward. He understood; and in fortitude and resignation he gave back to God his beautiful soul, a shining example of the priest, *alter Christus*.

This book, which depicts for us the priestly figure of Cardinal Stritch and describes with particular attention his priestly activities, will do much good. It will be warmly welcomed by those who had the good fortune to know the late lamented Cardinal.

A. G. CARD. CICOGNANI

Rome
April, 1959

ACKNOWLEDGMENTS

WITH deep gratitude the author begs to acknowledge the kindness of all those who have in any way contributed to the fashioning of THE CARDINAL STRITCH STORY, especially His Eminence, Cardinal Cicognani; Their Excellencies Archbishop O'Brien of Chicago; Archbishop Alter of Cincinnati; Archbishop O'Boyle of Washington, D. C.; Bishop Hayes of Davenport; Bishop Atkielski of Milwaukee; Bishop Hillinger of Chicago; Msgr. Hardiman; Msgr. Fitzgerald; Msgr. Casey; Msgr. Merlin Kearney of Memphis, Tenn.; Msgr. Tanner and Rev. John Cronin, S.S. of the N.C.W.C., Washington, D. C.; Msgr. Wycislo of the National Catholic War Relief; Msgr. Koenig; Msgr. Terlecke; Msgr. Dailey; Msgr. Kelly of the Chicago New World; Msgr. Kinnane, Tiffin, Ohio; Msgr. Max Walz, Perrysburg, Ohio; Rev. James O'Neill, S.J.; Rev. Father Bruggemann, S.J., of Mundelein Seminary; Rev. Ernest Burrus, S.J., of Rome; Rev. Raymond Prindiville, C.S.P.; Rev. Charles Burton Mouton, Papal Nunciature, India; Rev. Morris Stritch of Memphis, Tenn.; Rev. Richard Wojcik; Sister M. Alacoque, O.S.F.; Rev. Mother Regan, R.S.C.J.; Mr. Eugene Stritch, Nashville, Tenn.; Mr. Dan Ryan; Mr. Eugene Murphy; Miss Catherine Schaefer, UN (N.C.W.C.); Miss Johanna Doniat; Mrs. Marie Louise Charvet; Miss Mary Clifford.

THE CARDINAL STRITCH STORY

THE Pope was speaking. And the Pope was Pius X. His tired eyes lit into life as they looked upon eighteen expectant faces, the newly ordained students from the North American College, gathered for a farewell audience on this twenty-first day of May, 1910.

They had drawn close to the gentle Pontiff during the years of study in Rome. In addition to other occasions, he had received them always on the eighth of December, the feast of Mary Immaculate to whom their country was dedicated. More than ever, on this day of parting, the secret of his saintliness seemed to exercise its quiet influence upon them, and the new life opening before them caught added fire from the light that glowed in his words as he addressed them.

"*Benjamini miei!*" he cried out, while all the tenderness of a great, warm soul flowed into his voice. "My Benjamins! Come back, come back to Rome! You may not find this poor old Pope; but you will find another dressed in white and it will be just the same."

For one of the Benjamins, the youngest of them all, these words became a permanent possession. Samuel Stritch, with the oil of the priesthood fresh upon his hands at twenty-two, was to recall them many a time in the years to come and their overtones would linger strangely in the sounding of his hour of destiny.

One by one the young priests were presented to His Holiness. One by one they felt the reassuring pressure of his hand. When Samuel Stritch saw the benign eyes resting upon him, his heart went out forever to this gentle Pontiff, one of the great popes of all time, who

1

had come into his priestly life at its dawn and was to remain an undying influence until its end.

In his own vivid words the later Cardinal describes the unforgettable impression. "You felt," he recalls, "that you were in the presence of one who, to see you, had just stepped out of the presence of God."

II

ALTHOUGH Samuel Stritch was born in Nashville, Tennessee, it was not only the gracious Southland that entered into his fashioning. His father, Garrett Stritch, educated in Dublin, came from a family which, even in Catholic Ireland, was distinguished for loyalty to the Church long before 1651 when Cromwell, storming over the land, had one of its members executed in Limerick. The times were troubled for patriots when Garrett Stritch was young. In the 1870's he came to America and went by river steamer to Louisville, Kentucky, where he had a cousin.

It was there that he met and married Katherine Malley, American born, of Irish descent. There also the lifelong friendship with Major Lewis and his family began, and it was through the Major's influence that the Stritch family moved to Tennessee, into the industrial colony at Sycamore Mills in Cheatham County. Here the valiant spirit of faith that was in Katherine Stritch had the opportunity to manifest itself. The nearest Catholic church was in Nashville. To get there in time for Sunday Mass the family had to leave home on Saturday, travel by boat or by horse-drawn stage, spend the night in a hotel, and stay over until Monday to take the first stage home. The journey was not only strenuous, but expensive, and Katherine Stritch, unwilling to bring up her five children under such conditions, told her husband in her determined way, that he must move to a city where there was a Catholic church.

Garrett Stritch took his family back to Louisville; but after six months Major Lewis offered him the position of manager of the Nashville office of the Sycamore Mills plant, a subsidiary of Du Pont. In the rambling gray frame house with the high, arched windows and the small front yard, at 1121 Fifth Avenue corner of Madison, North Nashville, on August 17, 1887, Samuel Stritch was born. He was baptized in the Church of the Assumption which, to the joy of his mother, was only three blocks away.

For a little girl of three, living next door, this date became immortalized. In 1956 she wrote to Cardinal Stritch: "Dear Sam: Every year at this time I plan to send you a birthday letter; and every year it is crowded out of the day's agenda by my innumerable duties. . . . Did I ever tell you that perhaps my earliest recollection is of the night of August 17, 1887? I was sitting in my mother's lap on our front porch. Mother loved the soothing summer darkness after her busy day, and there were never any lamps burning in our house, until bedtime came. I am sure now that her thoughts were with her neighbor as we sat there so quietly, and that she was full of friendly concern. Anyway, someone came . . . a messenger, I don't at all remember who it was . . . and told us that a baby boy had arrived next door. I was nearly four years old, but if I have any memory that antedates this one, I do not identify it."

The same reminiscent writer draws a lifelike picture of Katherine Stritch: "I remember your little mother very vividly. I wonder if I have told you the story. . . . I heard it from my mother many times. It seems that I was sick one night . . . my mother had no experience with croup. Then my father came home, and the legend has it that as he walked in the door and heard my struggles to breathe, he exclaimed in horror 'My God! That child has the croup!' The next step seems to have been an SOS to the good neighbor. . . . your mother came at once, and took charge, expertly. She prepared the hot poultices, or whatever was the right remedy, and as she worked she prayed aloud, and as she prayed she kept on working. My mother was always sure that I owed my life to that timely help. And to this hour I remember it with gratitude.

"I like to remember too how pretty she was, with her delicate features, brown eyes, and black hair. . . . I recall too that as a little girl I thought there was nothing so delicious as her sweet pickled peaches . . . and she always saved a jar for me when she 'put up' peaches in the summer. Do you remember how wonderful was the vegetable soup at your house . . . midsummer soup with all the fresh vegetables? When have you ever eaten anything as good as that was?"

Years later when Samuel Stritch had become a cardinal, his memory lingered lovingly over the dawn of his life of which he himself tells the story: "I have so many happy memories of my childhood in Nashville, that it would be impossible to single out any one. Nashville was simple back in those days: We enjoyed ourselves without any artificial amusements. We played baseball and marbles and flew our kites, just as they came along, each in its season."

There seems to have been a wholesome balance of work and play for the eight Stritch children, of whom Samuel was the second youngest. "There was no central heating," his brother testifies, and since there were plenty of chores, "Sam did his share of bringing the kindling and coal for all of the fireplaces and stoves." He did not begin school until he was seven; but he learned so quickly that he was soon two grades beyond other boys of his age. One of his teachers tells of a day when she assigned eleven problems in arithmetic, so difficult that she did not expect the class to solve many of them; but she gave them a choice and promised ten points for every correct answer. And Samuel's grade was 110.

"He was terribly bright," an old friend asserts; but his brother gives assurance that he worked no harder at his studies than did the average boy. "He was as conscientious as any of the rest of us," his brother says, "about saying his daily prayers, but not more so. But as he grew older, he became more interested in the Church. I don't think there ever was any doubt in his mind about what he would do."

It is consequently evident that although the signs of a brilliant intelligence were unmistakable and there were pronounced hints of his later intensity of devotion to the Church, no outer pressures beyond the normal forced these qualities into functioning. With young Sammy everything came in an easy, natural manner. Had there been anything of the prig about him or any atom of stuffiness in his make-up, his classmates would not have liked him as they did, nor would his big brothers have been so willing to take him with them when they went swimming in White's Creek. He was, on the contrary, as mischievous as he was bright, quick at play, easy to get along with.

He was still a very small boy at Assumption School when his teacher, Sister Catherine, having left the classroom for a few minutes one day, returned to find the atmosphere permeated with the fragrance of oranges. "Who has eaten an orange?" she inquired forthwith. No one answered. She thereupon walked up and down the aisle asking every child whether he had eaten an orange. Invariably the answer was "No." "Someone is not telling the truth," Sister Catherine insisted. Then Sammy Stritch, her prize pupil, raised his hand. "Sister," he said, with serious blue eyes fixed intently upon her, "I did not eat an orange. I ate half an orange."

When he was scarcely nine years old the first shock of sorrow came with the death of his father in 1896. It was well for Katherine Stritch, left alone with the care of a large family, that she was a strong-willed, valiant woman, kind but firm, as one of her sons characterized her. The devotedness of her children however, the spirit of sacrifice awakened by the inevitably changed conditions, lightened the burdens of her untimely widowhood. With loving reminiscence Cardinal Stritch tells of an instance of the children's solicitude for the comfort of their mother. They wanted to buy her something very special for Christmas and for many eager months saved their pennies for the grand surprise. The bulky package was opened at last and when a handsome footstool emerged, there were tears in the eyes of Katherine Stritch.

To the end of his days Samuel was to carry the memory of his mother as the most precious of his life. "My mother," he said, "was, of course, the greatest influence in my life. She, more than anyone else, was responsible for the decisions of my life."

From the Assumption School Samuel Stritch transferred to St. Mary's and every Sunday he ran up the hill to serve Mass at St. Mary's Cathedral. Its rector, Father John Morris, later Bishop of Little Rock, became the second great influence in the shaping of his career. The eventual marriage of Ellen, sister of Father Morris, to Samuel's brother, Thomas, established a further bond between them. Years later, Cardinal Stritch said that Father Morris was "next to my mother, the most influential person in my life. He had a great deal to do with my early interest in going into the Church."

This interest, grown to a conviction and a love, drew Samuel Stritch away from home to St. Gregory's Preparatory Seminary in Cincinnati after having finished his high school course at the age of fourteen. He left Nashville, a slender, dark-haired boy, small for his age, in short trousers, black stockings, high-topped shoes, and wearing a bow tie. As such it is easy to picture him giving a good account of himself in the leading part of a play at St. Gregory's as Little Lord Fauntleroy.

The childhood promise of extraordinary intelligence continued to fulfill itself at St. Gregory's and he brought to this new academic life a mind stored with well-directed reading. Of this the Cardinal himself gave an account in an interview granted to Mr. Dan Herr, and published in *Books on Trial.* "I recall," he said, "that reading in my family was so common a practice that the children one by one got into it without conscious effort. My father was the son of a Kerry schoolteacher and had more than the ordinary education of his associates. He kindled in all of us a love of good books. My mother, after her day's work, could be seen in the evening with a book. I think too that all those in our neighborhood identified good reading with good manners.

"At school it was drilled into us that education came in the main through good reading. But our reading was supervised. I remember getting my first public library card when I was about twelve. The lady at the library was very careful about the books given to children. Still, one day somehow I did get hold of a book which seemed to me a promising bit of fiction. When my mother saw it, she quietly took it away and next day I got another book from the library."

He tells of reading *Robinson Crusoe, Treasure Island, Arabian Nights,* and others. At one time he found the Indian stories of James Fennimore Cooper enchanting. Then came Washington Irving, the American poets, and much of Poe. He read Scott's novels and poetry, Thackeray, some Bulwer Lytton. "Shakespeare," he said, "was a must for everybody and when Shakespearean players came to our town, it was an event and we saved our pennies for the admission fee. It was the day of romanticism and even in popular literature there were many good nice things for us to read. I know romanticism is out of style, but I am glad it had an influence on me."

It is consequently not surprising that when Samuel Stritch went to boarding school, literature was his favorite study. He tells how eagerly he studied the Dr. Johnson period, and that he slowly turned from fiction and poetry to history and biography.

The Cardinal shed further light on the tastes of his early youth when asked whether poetry had been an important part of his reading. "At one time in my life," he admits, "I was greatly interested in poetry and eagerly read our English poets. It may be that I missed much in them in my immaturity, but they delighted me no end. . . . What a pity it is that if a great poet in our country came today, he would have a hard time finding a publisher. There can be no real literature without poetry. Sometimes I think that the trouble happened when some later poets tried to tell in poetry what only music can tell and became unintelligible to ordinary folk. Then too it seems to me that with the coming of the modern critic, studies of poetry became overrationalized. There may be something in Browning's remark, when asked the meaning of one of his verses: 'I do not remember.' "

Reading always remained something fundamental in the life and thinking of Samuel Stritch. Just as he has said that habits of reading remain, but your particular interests in life come to influence your choices in reading, so by the same token, as his interests multiplied and his insight deepened, his concept of reading grew into implications much more vitally associated with human living than even its identification with good manners. Later in his career when the intensity of his interest in education ranged far beyond the boundaries of his own personality, he saw even in the basic techniques of learning to read, a far-reaching significance, as the following letter reveals. On June 1, 1955, he wrote to a friend associated with a publishing house:

"I thank you for your letter of May 24th, in which you tell me how much you appreciate what we are doing to better the teaching of reading in our schools and to help those who are defective in their reading. For many years I have realized two things; namely, that elementary school education depends very much upon success in teaching the child to read and, secondly, that bad reading habits and difficulties in reading have a very close connection with bad behavior problems. When we started this work here in Chicago there wasn't all the publicity which there is now in the country about poor reading and the need for remedial reading clinics. We went at it because we saw the problem. Really we have received great encouragement and there is a great deal of interest in our teachers. During the summer we hope to do something significant in expanding our program and doing the thing in our schools which will make them correspond with their high ideals."

During the two years at St. Gregory's the vision of the priesthood grew steadily stronger to Samuel Stritch. With it the desire for Rome, the city of the Pope, had begun to root itself in his heart. His stay at boarding school had been unbroken by any vacation at home. The eyes of Bishop Byrne of Nashville were upon him and when, after receiving his bachelor degree, Samuel returned, the Bishop had made a decision. It was to be Rome, and in its North American College his promising young student would complete his studies for the priesthood. The Bishop was laying a cornerstone into the life of Samuel Stritch; and into the shaping of his career, the third great influence had come.

At the news, however, the face of Katherine Stritch did not reflect the radiance in the eyes of her son. He was only sixteen. She looked at him, slight and frail as he stood before her. She could not let him travel alone to Rome. She could not let him live so far away for six long years. In her distress she pleaded with him, she refused her consent, only to encounter a will, gently expressed, yet strong as her own. To be almost too sensitive to giving pain to others was part of the character of Samuel Stritch. And this was his mother!

But the call of Rome was strong. "Mother," he said, and the word came like a caress, "don't you know that it's a sin to interfere with one's vocation?" There was a hint of jest in his voice; but the note of finality was in it. For this Katherine Stritch had no reply. The fullness of a blessing emerged from her heart as she let him go, the boy who would not return until he was a priest.

III

THE eyes of Samuel Stritch were wide with wonder as the big liner steamed into the Bay of Naples. Geography alive and full of color! To the right stood famed Vesuvius with a thin white cloud over its flattened crown, and the two silent cities, Pompeii and

Herculaneum, in its menacing shadow. Amalfi, Sorrento, and other small white cities hung enchantingly over the cliffs in the brilliant sunshine. To the left towered a building, the color of rose.

The goal was nearing. This was but the entrance. Lovely as it was, the young student with the light in his eyes and the vision in his heart had no desire to linger on the way to Rome. But the sun was on its downward course, leaving behind a pink and gold sky streaked with the purple shadows of approaching darkness. It was evening when the steamer docked and he came down the gangplank and made his way through customs. He would have to spend the night in Naples, so he hailed one of the ever ready cabbies and gave the name of the hotel which Bishop Byrne had recommended. The cabby drove through street after street, reaching the hotel at last with a weary young passenger. The next morning when Sammy came out of the front door he saw to his amazement that the steamer he had left was just across the street. But he was going to Rome. Nothing else mattered very much.

Friendly Italians sharing the compartment on the train smiled at the little Americano sitting close to the window while orange trees, vineyards, and the columns of ruined aqueducts swept by. He knew that midway between Naples and Rome, but too far inland to see, St. Benedict's ancient monastery was standing like a fortress on its mountaintop. He would visit it some day. Six years was a long time; but scarcely long enough for all that Samuel Stritch hoped to do.

The train stood still. It was the Eternal City! And through the bustle of arrival an American voice calling: "Hello, there you are!" A warm American handclasp followed and he was at home.

Bishop Kennedy, rector of the North American College on the Via Umiltà looked with surprise and a kindly smile at the slight figure in knickerbockers standing before him, more like an acolyte than a seminarian. The boy was shy; but the manners of the southern gentleman did not fail him and he spoke with the soft intonations of his native Tennessee. The straightforward answers, the quick responses in his eyes did not escape the rector. Bishop Byrne had made no mistake, he commented inwardly. This boy will make good.

Joyously Samuel Stritch put on the black cassock with the blue buttons, white collar, and red cincture, the red, white, and blue of his country. In the chapel where the light is always mellow, where at the rear, low on the left wall, Christ Crucified hangs white and bloodstained, he set out upon his eager journey to the priesthood, an offering to God, to Rome, and to America.

Although his classmates soon became aware of the intellectual stature of Samuel Stritch, to them he was "Little Sammy," of whom the late Bishop Griffin of Springfield, a classmate and throughout his life a faithful friend, has left us a charming picture.

"I first met the Cardinal of Chicago," he writes, "on a cool October evening in 1904. I saw him standing beside the portico of the Villa Santa Caterina, the summer home of the students of Rome's North American College, 18 miles south of the Eternal City, in the Alban Hills.

"He was wearing knickerbockers. Some of us thought he might be a visiting high school tourist. He certainly seemed too young to be a seminarian. He was frail and quiet. He held out his hand and said: 'My name's Stritch. What's yours?'

"Shaking hands with him, I told him my name, that I was from Chicago's far-famed South Side. I learned that he was from Nashville, and as he continued to speak in his soft manner, that he was my classmate at the university in Rome.

"It seems ludicrous now, but I must confess I felt sorry for this hopeful neophyte. How could he ever weather the rigors of seminary life in Rome, where hot water was something to read about in physics class but never seen, where the food was something unheard of at Henrici's Restaurant in Chicago, and the Lord help the one who couldn't subsist on platters of spaghetti and olive oil.

"I still count it somewhat of a miracle that young Stritch of Nashville was the only one in my class who braved more than six years of Roman life without even being sick a day."

IV

QUIETLY and cheerfully Samuel Stritch settled into life at the North American College. The students lived together in the intimacy of brothers. In the Roman winter when marble floors added to the chill of unheated corridors they froze together. When the summer sun beat upon them they burned together. But they worked together toward their common objective, walking day by day in small groups through the narrow, stone streets toward the College of the Propaganda.

It is significant to remember that in 1904 when Samuel Stritch went to Rome, America was still a missionary country and the North American students took their classes in the College of the Propaganda. This venerable building is close to one of the most attractive squares of the city, the Piazza Spagna with the Madonna standing on her tall column at the center, and the wide sweep of the Spanish stairs leading up the Pincian Hill to the famous old Church of the Trinita dei Monti and the adjoining Convent of the Sacred Heart.

Life moves in gala tempo about the ancient fountain and among the glowing colors of flower stands at the base of the hill. Here in the early Roman spring there is compensation for all the gnawing dampness of winter, when the vines and trellises burst into flower and the great stairway is lined with azaleas that give the impression of enormous hanging gardens so that one can but look, exclaim, and stop breathing for one rapturous moment. There was much to lighten the burden of study while walking the streets of Rome. At every little interval, from wall or street corner, or unsuspected nook, the face of the Madonna looks down upon the passer-by. Broken columns, carved façades, storytelling stones thrill the imagination with the mystery of the past.

To these mute teachers the inner ear of Samuel Stritch was attuned. While attaining to his degree first in philosophy, then in theology, he developed two absorbing hobbies peculiarly fitted to Rome. One was Church history; the other, Christian archaeology. Avidly he read Pastor's *History of the Popes* from beginning to end. As for archaeology, every inch of Rome ministered to his interest. The old churches are legion. He not only visited them, but he studied them, making profitable use of the hours of freedom in the late afternoons when priest, friar, student, and the populace of Rome emerge from the hours of siesta and the business of the city resumes the life of the morning.

Though classes may be over for the day, all Rome is a challenge to the student whose inner senses are keen; for under its crowded streets a silent city lies and hour by hour one walks upon the buried centuries. To Samuel Stritch the Appian Way had grown familiar. With untiring energy he followed the steep and stony paths down into the earth where the early Christians lie, and so well did he master the twists and turnings that as time went on he was permitted to go through the catacombs without a guide.

His hours of recreation, however, were not confined to burrowings into the past. He was a great walker and with other students frequently went on long hikes through the Italian countryside and far up into the neighboring hills. There were holiday times too, when students had the opportunity to visit some of the other cities of Italy. It was probably the visit to Florence that stimulated Samuel Stritch's love of Dante which remained with him throughout his life.

After Samuel's first year in Rome he was appointed third sacristan because of his piety. The following year he was second sacristan, and the third year he became first sacristan. This work was always a joy to him. He would spend hours polishing candlesticks, and many a time when other students were outdoors he would be down in the dreary grease room, as it was called, paring candles. He had become what the students named a "greaser," and though his knuckles cracked with the cold on winter days, he was uncomplaining and his ready smile did not fail. Reminiscently he smiled again in 1946 when he went to Rome to receive the cardinal's red hat, visited the North American College, and sought out his old haunt, the sacristy. "I don't think they shine candlesticks as well as we did," he said with a sly little gleam in the corner of his eye. He delighted in telling of the time, also associated with the sacristy, when he was expelled from the North American College. The rector came down one morning to the lower chapel where Sammy and three others were in charge of the sacristy and, finding something wrong, told them that they were all expelled and that he would write to every seminary in America to see that they were not accepted. Apparently they did not consider themselves guilty; for they went in to see him after breakfast to tell him how he had hurt their feelings. His reply was: "I was feeling bad this morning. Now you may go out 'in black' today." Going out in black was a special privilege.

Though James Griffin, later bishop of Springfield, and Martin Hayden, afterward monsignor, were perhaps his closest friends, Samuel mingled freely and pleasantly with all the students. He loved the college and was interested in most of its activities. He was an excellent handball player and an inveterate walker. When the so-called Horribles and Terribles played a match at baseball, he was the first choice for the team of the Horribles.

Often, during the summer holidays at the Villa Caterina in the lovely Alban Hill country, while other students were busy at a game of tennis, Samuel Stritch could be found sitting under a tree reading his Pastor's *History of the Popes*. During this time at their summer villa the North American students had occasion to become more closely acquainted with the Papal Secretary of State, Cardinal Merry del Val. It was he who always arranged their audiences with the Holy Father; but during the carefree days when he lived at neighboring Castel Gondolfo, he would come, sometimes twice a week, to play tennis with the boys. The Cardinal loved sports, frequently attended their games of football, and knew the students by their first names. Samuel Stritch admired and loved this glorious Cardinal and years later when speaking of him, he remembered that the impression he retained was not that of one predominating quality, but of a remarkable wholeness of personality.

At the end of two years Samuel Stritch received his doctorate in philosophy, and after four years of theology he became Doctor of Divinity. At the Propaganda he was recognized as an outstanding student, even among all the national groups, being, what we would call today, a straight "A" student. He was nevertheless to all appearances an ordinary, lively American collegian and seminarian respected by everyone.

"As a boy," one of his early friends relates, "he was a hard student. He profited much more than the average seminarian by his six years in Rome." Meanwhile he had learned to speak Italian fluently, to love Italy and Italians. Even Italian cooking — ministrone, ravioli, and the many kinds of pasta — had come to rank beside the favorite southern dishes: chicken pie, snap beans, turnip greens, and hominy grits. The Southland and home came very close on one occasion with a visit from Bishop Morris. "Sammy," said the Bishop, "come and get your hair cut." Evidently the later Cardinal's indifference toward haircuts had an early beginning. Perhaps even the fact that silver threads were slipping into his hair at the age of eighteen received scant, if any, attention.

The time of preparation was nearing its end, and on the Holy Thursday of 1910 a privilege was granted to Samuel Stritch which was a culminating point of all that had gone before and a preparation for all that was to come. His Holiness Pius X asked that six American students come to his private chapel for Mass at 6:30, and Samuel Stritch was one of the six. Since significant influences never lay dormant within the spirit of Samuel Stritch, we can believe in the enrichment that must have come when Christ, His Vicar who was a saint, and a dedicated youth met on a morning like Holy Thursday.

It was to Samuel's advantage during these fervent, garnering years, that he did not look upon Rome with the eyes of a visitor.

He was at home in this Eternal City. All the American students loved it. For him it entered into the blood stream, and he lived well on all that he saw and heard. With strange tongues sounding in his ears and the familiar sight of seminarians of other nations and races, and from far-flung mission fields, his mental vision sought widening horizons until it swept the distant margins of the earth. Daily his imagination was focused upon a picture of endless variety, with the transcendent unity that is the Church as its center.

Here in Rome one could feel the heartbeat of the Church. It was only in Rome that the silver trumpets heralded the presence of the Vicar of Christ. Here alone, at the great ceremonies in St. Peter's, all the Church Militant seemed to throng into its immensity, while Pius stood at the Altar of Confession above the tomb of Peter. Here, at the Elevation of the Mass, as only the Pope can do, the Sacred Host is uplifted toward the four corners of the world, circling slowly so as to encompass the earth in a global embrace. At that moment a tremendous reality grows visible insofar as it is possible to human eyes, the Reality of the Mystical Body of Christ.

This, according to the testimony of his later life, is what Rome meant to Samuel Stritch. From it his priesthood grew rich at the source and absorbed a quality peculiarly its own. The years were to prove beyond question that the more he received from Rome, the more he had to give to America and to the world.

V

SPRING had come to Rome again, and for the class of 1910, the day of ordination stood luminous within the approaching month of May. At the North American College the custom prevailed that the officers of the house with studies completed were ordained one year in advance of the required age. As sacristan Samuel Stritch was an officer; but because of his youth he could not be included in the privilege.

To relieve this handicap the rector, Bishop Kennedy, came to the rescue. He arranged for an audience with the Holy Father and took Samuel Stritch to the Vatican. A great hope burned in the heart of the young seminarian as he looked expectantly into the eyes of Pius X. The goal was so near and so uncertain.

He heard the voice of the rector saying: "Holy Father, here is a young man ready for ordination in everything but years. He is only twenty-two. What can we do about it?"

The Pope smiled into the eyes and into the soul of Samuel Stritch. "He is young in years," he replied without hesitation, "but old in intelligence. Ordain him."

On Trinity Sunday, the twenty-first of May, 1910, in the great mother church, the Basilica of St. John Lateran, Cardinal Respighi ordained Samuel Stritch to the priesthood. For him, the youngest of all the young priests, the opening words of the Mass seemed to apply with special significance: "I will go unto the altar of God, to God who giveth joy to my youth." There is likewise a fitting association of ideas in the fact that he offered his first Mass in the

17

church of the youthful St. Agnes with its adjoining catacombs, on the Via Nomentana where the child martyr once lived.

The six intense years were over now. The Pope had given his Benjamins a farewell blessing, and the class of 1910 was homeward bound. With quiet humor in his eye the spiritual director of the North American College, Bishop Farrelly, who was also of Nashville, gave his erstwhile seminarians a little parting talk. He told them that there was no more beautiful sight in the world than the Bay of Naples with Vesuvius, Pompeii, Ischya, the graceful shore line, all under a blue canopy of sky, viewed from the deck of a ship whose prow is pointed westward.

With gratitude in his heart young Father Stritch watched the shores of Italy recede before turning his glance or his thoughts toward the West. "Even more than the great value of my studies," he said many years later, "was the reality which Rome gave me of the catholicity of the Church. Seeing all nations and all races there in the center of Catholic life made a lasting impression on me. In Rome I realized, too, that there is a world outside the United States, although I never ceased to be fervently in love with my own country. The feeling I gained there of solidarity with people all over the world has never left me."

Following upon the six years in Rome, Father Stritch spent six years in parish work, first at the Church of the Assumption in Nashville, where he had been baptized. During this time he was also chaplain to the Little Sisters of the Poor. He then became assistant at St. Patrick's in Memphis, where he later replaced the pastor.

When he first arrived in Memphis, he had been assigned to a small community in the mountains. Before he could go, however, to work among these simple people of the hills, his orders were changed. When the mountaineers heard of this, they sent word that it was all right with them. They had been worried about a young man like him roaming around the mountains all alone. In Memphis a little touch of home came to him through the devoted colored woman, Mrs. Hodge, who had worked for his mother when he was a child, and who came to be his housekeeper at his new post. Her little daughter, Agatha, was possibly the first baby, at least the first colored child, that he baptized. This child was to be devoted to him throughout his life.

Busy as Father Stritch was during these early years of ministry in larger cities, his thoughts, for some unexplained reason, turned longingly to a little town in Tennessee, called Cleveland. Far from looking toward the higher ranges of ecclesiastical position for which his natural gifts and his training had fitted him, his ambitions were focused upon this little corner where he could have worked among the Negroes and the poor. While he was aiming to persuade the Bishop to appoint him to a "nice little parish" in Cleveland, obedience pointed in a different direction when, in 1916, Bishop Byrne summoned him to Nashville to be his secretary. Other duties were added during the ensuing few years. Father Stritch became chancellor of the diocese, superintendent of schools, and pastor of the Cathedral.

The experiences of both pastoral life and administrative activity were crowded into the early years of priesthood, and here the paradox within the character of Samuel Stritch began to be revealed: inner enthusiasm expressed itself in outward calm; activity at white heat lived side by side with serenity; complexity, woven as it was, by some hidden magic, formed itself into a design of utter simplicity. With the ease with which a man fills one position, Samuel Stritch discharged the duties of four. The vicar-general of Nashville, Monsignor Siener, said of him: "I have never seen a man who could do so many jobs well."

To understand the later development of his meteoric career one must at the outset try to penetrate to the unifying force at the core of a lifetime of multiple functioning. Sometimes the end of a life supplies the key to its beginnings. Sometimes it is the small spontaneous human act strewn here and there in the background of a strenuous public career that divulges the secret of a man's soul. It is

this secret that is worth seeking as one surveys the lifework of someone who has contributed much to his period in the history of the
world.

In this connection the German writer, Emil Ludwig, has some
significant things to say. On the subject of "genius and character"
in an introduction to the writing of history he quotes Plutarch's
words: "I record not history, but human destiny." He refers to the
discovery of a human soul as the constant problem. "God is expert,"
he says, "and has always imbued the course of His creatures' lives
with a deeper logic than even the most skilled constructor can in-
vent. Often the time, the nature and the circumstances of a death
determine the interpretation of all preceding events . . . the most
trivial habit will often suggest the interpretation for some major
trait of character. The aim is to define that unchanging substance
of which these qualities are but the varying aspects. As we sense the
logic of our own life, similarly we will observe with awe the logic
of other destinies and will interpret cautiously the past recorded
on that complicated tapestry of human characters in which the
hand of God is manifest."

The life and character of Samuel Stritch is a tapestry woven of
many strands; but the one golden thread at the center of each
design, the one upon which the character of the whole texture depends, seems unquestionably to be his priesthood in all that it
implies. From it the efforts of his life derived their inspiration. In
it his natural gifts and extraordinary talents found their fullest expression. Through it his supernatural life grew to its destined stature.

Of this, Rome apparently was not unaware. In the May of 1921
Pope Benedict XV named him a Domestic Prelate. The subsequent
question was: Why not a bishop? In August of the same year the
Pope appointed him Bishop of Toledo.

One of the first to congratulate him was his old friend and classmate of Roman days, Father William Murphy of the archdiocese of
Chicago. The latter's surprise at the news equaled, perhaps, that of
a day in 1904 when, sitting in his room at the North American
College in Rome, there was a sudden knock at his door. He called

"Come in," and a frail boy of sixteen stood before him with the simple introduction. "I am Stritch from Nashville."

And "Stritch from Nashville," the Bishop-elect of Toledo, was true to his inclinations when he confided to his friend: "I only wish that they would leave me with my books and studies. . . ."

As time proved, he was destined never to be "left" with anything. Although he was a born scholar, and would have loved being a teacher of philosophy, this inclination became part of a greater love: the Church, the love of his life, in the service of which all inclinations and aptitudes were to be both used and sacrificed.

VI

"WHERE do you come from, young man?" The elderly chaplain of the convent looked with interest at the young priest with the smiling, intelligent eyes who had come to Cincinnati to participate in the jubilee celebration of one of the Sisters. "From Nashville," the young priest replied. The chaplain looked up in surprise. Ohio was interested in the bishop newly appointed for Toledo, but not yet installed. He was to come from Nashville.

"Tell me," the chaplain inquired, "what about that young whippersnapper who is to be bishop of Toledo? What sort of a person is he? And what is the Church coming to, sending a boy for a bishop?"

The young priest of thirty-four who did not look his age replied with his most gracious smile: "I can't tell you much about him, Father; but I think he means well."

"By the way," the chaplain asked while bidding his guest good night, "I haven't asked you your name."

Again the ingratiating smile while a merry twinkle appeared in the young priest's blue eyes and the drawl of Tennessee lingered melodiously over the name as he replied: "Stritch."

In Toledo the lights burned later than usual in the Church of St. Francis de Sales on the eve of St. Andrew's day. With suppressed excitement the priests were arranging the vestments for the new Bishop who was to be consecrated on the following day. With amazement they handled the shoes, wondering how they could be so small and how they would fit into the footsteps of his predecessor, Bishop Schrembs.

For Samuel Stritch it meant the fitting into an entirely new pattern of life. It meant the severing of the ties of home, leaving the loved South for the different ways of the North. It meant taking upon his youthful shoulders a shepherd's burden that would be for life.

Later in his episcopal career he said almost apologetically: "I was only a boy then." Although at his consecration on November 30, 1921, he became the youngest member of the hierarchy, it was not long before an elderly monsignor said one day: "When I talk to him I feel that he is older than I am." It was likewise not long before those who had prepared the Bishop's vestments and marveled at the small shoes came to the conclusion that the footgear had little relationship to the size of the ideas which occupied his mind and even less to the breadth of the virtues that made themselves felt in the form of a great human warmth and kindness.

Toledo was a young diocese. At its head was the youngest of bishops. They grew up together. Life was vibrant and full of promise. The preceding years had prepared Bishop Stritch both in his pastoral and administrative capacity. Now the time of vision was at hand. The opportunity to develop a creative ability was in the offing. The dynamic first Bishop of Toledo had laid foundations that were deep and strong. With all his natural aptitudes and supernatural resources the second Bishop began to build upon them. Young as he was, the new dignity did not change him. The unaccustomed pomp that inevitably went with his office served but to emphasize his essential simplicity and selflessness. His brilliant mental qualities, his gift of thinking intuitively, in balance with the counterpull of acting with deliberation and prudence, functioned unimpeded because there was nothing of self in them.

He settled easily into the happy, peaceful years at 2544 Parkwood Avenue while his secretary began to make discoveries concerning him. He took note of the extraordinary memory for factual data, for the names of persons, even of those whom he met only casually. Faces he might forget; but names and circumstances remained clear in his mind. The secretary observed that the Bishop was a hard worker who did not tire either under ceremonies or preaching. He knew of his love for reading and that reading was his recreation. Apropos of recreation he once heard the Bishop say: "All the average priest needs is a smoke, a newspaper, and a bishop to talk about."

As for cigarettes, the Bishop, in times of stress, was known to light one cigarette after another and throw them aside. In Toledo, he must have "rolled his own," for it remains in the memory of his housekeeper's daughter that as a little girl nothing fascinated her so much as to see the Bishop rolling a cigarette. The same little girl had pet mice and loves to recall how the Bishop used to help her decorate them with red ribbons.

Vividly the secretary remembers the Bishop going to his typewriter after office appointments; for he typed many letters himself. Frequently when the doorbell rang the Bishop answered it and when callers came he received them, seldom requiring an appointment for the giving of interviews. No appointment was required for the old German who came in one day with an extraordinary complaint: "Our pastor," he said, "has bought one of them electric iceboxes. When he had a regular icebox he paid for the ice. Now who is going to pay for his electricity? Do we have to?"

The Bishop saw that this case needed a little diplomacy. "Oh, has he a new refrigerator?" he asked. "Have you seen it?" "No, Bishop."

Bishop Stritch then asked his visitor to come to the kitchen with him. He interested the man so thoroughly in the refrigerator that when the Bishop asked, "Don't you think your wife would like one?" the man thought maybe she would.

In the evening, when there were no engagements, there was always a walk, from Parkwood Avenue to Monroe, sometimes farther, and back on Scottwood. The walking habits of Roman days had not changed, and the Bishop was a pace-setter for any companion.

This was routine; but enterprise was close beside it. In the late afternoon Mark the chauffeur was at hand to drive the Bishop to building sites or to explore for new locations. His consuming interest in Catholic education manifested itself during his first year as Ordinary of Toledo. That education is the first charity of the Church, was his firm conviction.

In 1922, with the opening of the diocesan Mary Manse College, higher education, under the direction of the Ursulines, was made possible for women, within a short distance of home. In 1923 he established Calvert High School in Tiffin, Ohio, and in the same year consolidated all diocesan mission projects into a central Home and Foreign Mission office. In 1924 he unified all the charitable activities of the diocese under the Toledo Catholic Charities, Incorporated.

With his continuous preoccupation with education and his usual insight he realized that in order to produce good schools and satisfactory students the first requirement is to supply competent teachers. He accordingly opened Teachers' College in 1924, for the training of Sisters and lay teachers. This was the first diocesan teachers' college in the country and it operates with full-time sessions, summer sessions, and extension courses.

In the following year he inaugurated a drive for a central Catholic high school. For this purpose he drew upon his abounding confidence in Mary's intercession. His eye was upon a certain building site on Cherry Street, which others also wanted. He therefore led a crusade of prayer, and though he had to wait for it, his request was finally granted. The cornerstone was laid in 1928 and when it came to the staffing of the school, the Bishop carried out an idea that at the time was entirely original. He formed a teaching faculty from members of various communities, thereby creating the first high school of its kind in the United States. Today this institution has an enrollment of more than one thousand boys.

In all his undertakings the Bishop was receiving remarkable co-operation from his clergy. He had come almost as a stranger, knowing only three priests, two from Roman days and one from the college in Cincinnati. But his friendliness quickly put him in touch with every priest in the diocese.

There were others also: there were the people who came to his door, who experienced not only his friendliness but his generosity and his unsuspecting charity. On one memorable evening he was called to the parlor to see a woman who was in distress. She lived in an apartment with her little daughter, her rent was in arrears, and unless she had $20 at once, she would be evicted. "Well, if you have nothing, how about food?" the Bishop asked. "We will get along somehow," she replied.

He had two twenty-dollar bills and a fifty-cent piece in his pocket. He insisted upon her accepting the forty dollars. That night a burglar broke into the house, got to the Bishop's room, and took the fifty cents.

Whether or not the harsher northern climate was responsible, Bishop Stritch suffered, and sometimes severely, from a sinus condition; but it seldom interrupted the steady drive of his routine. "I didn't get warm that first year until August," he confided to a friend. During one of the winters when an attack of sinus trouble was particularly severe, the Bishop decided to go to Florida. Some of his priests accompanied him. One sunny day while out walking they happened to pass a barber shop. By this time it was a well-established fact that, whether in Toledo or in Florida, the Bishop consistently ignored his need of a haircut. At sight of the barber shop one of the priests thought he had found a way to remedy the matter with consummate diplomacy. "Guess I'll stop in and get a haircut," he remarked quite casually. The Bishop smiled his ever ready smile and promptly replied: "I'll go with you — and get a shine."

Although the Bishop did not become acclimated to northern winters and usually kept his room at a panting temperature of eighty degrees, the North made compensation in the joy that it gave him, after the sparse Catholic settlements in the South, to find so many flourishing country parishes in the vicinity of Toledo. In the city itself the Bishop established seven new parishes during his stay of nine years. But year after year he continued his appeal for more priests and more Sisters.

Meanwhile the year 1925 had come and left its indelible impression. It was the Holy Year and the call of Rome was strong. It was his first return to the city that for six epochal years had been his home and he celebrated it by leading a pilgrimage for the Holy Year. It was doubly a pilgrimage, a pilgrimage of grace to the appointed sacred places, and a pilgrimage of reminiscence, visiting again the haunts that he knew and loved in the receding student days.

He returned with a dream in his heart. Toledo was maturing as a diocese. It deserved a magnificent cathedral and before 1925 had passed the project began to take form. In 1926, a crowning enterprise and a supreme dedication to our Lady, the Bishop undertook the building of the Cathedral of the Holy Rosary. On the twenty-fifth of June Cardinal Reig and Casanova, archbishop of Toledo in Spain, visited Bishop Stritch of Toledo in America. He saw the beginning of the cathedral and pointed out that it was exactly 700 years since the cornerstone of the Cathedral of Toledo in Spain, was laid. Two days later, on June 27, Cardinal Czernock, Primate of Hungary, laid the cornerstone of the Cathedral of the Holy Rosary.

One might conclude that the Bishop had reason to be highly gratified by the results of his labors; but, as we can see from the following annual letter written in 1926, his desires were directed rather to an increase in the piety of his people.

"We feel sore at heart," he wrote, "to notice, especially in our cities, that the number attending evening devotions is so very small. Very fast we are becoming merely a Mass-going Catholic people. The shorter the instruction even on Sunday, the greater seems to be the crowd. There is no thirst for the Word of God."

He was not destined to write another annual letter to the people of Toledo. He was not destined to witness the completion of the Cathedral. The year 1930 had come.

VII

IT WAS autumn in Toledo. On a chill November evening five thousand of its citizens, Catholics and non-Catholics, were streaming into the Civic Auditorium for a farewell dinner to its Bishop. No longer the stranger from the South, he was a possession that Toledo had hoped to keep. He was now forty-three years old and had fully believed that he would live and die in this his first diocese. But Rome had other plans and on August 26 he was appointed Archbishop of Milwaukee. How certain he was that in Toledo he would find his last resting place we can infer from a letter written on March 9, 1930, to a nun of the Convent of the Visitation in Toledo.

"I want to thank you and the Sisters belatedly but cordially for your kindness in granting my request to be buried in your vault below the Chapel. This is a favor that I treasure highly and that I cannot repay. My Visitation is always for greatest joy and consolation. There I want to rest in death where a daily prayer for me shall go up before God Who is *Praestabilis super malitia*. Let them place no monument over me, for if when death comes I shall have failed to erect in the lives of my people a monument before God, of what avail shall words graven in stone be? I want to forbid any violation of the cloister rule on the occasion of my funeral. Just let the usual ministers take me into the cloister to wait the Angel's call. Do not permit them to mock me with fine words and costly finery, but say to them to shroud me with prayers and give their alms to the poor. One only thing do I request of the Sisters and that is: If ever my Visitation should cease to be strictly of the Visitation observance, on that day I want my body taken and carried over among the poor at Calvary. While I wait among the Sisters for the Resurrection, I shall try always to call to them: Caritas, Caritas, Caritas."

In 1929, Bishop Stritch had paid his *ad limina* visit to Rome. It was then that Monsignor Kinnane, the friend who accompanied him, sensed the respect that he inspired among those in authority, and was therefore not surprised when, after the death of Archbishop Messmer of Milwaukee, the new appointment came.

The Bishop himself, far from being elated at the promotion, met it with obedience and a heartache. After he was in Milwaukee he told this same friend: "I didn't want to leave Toledo at all. But I had the experience of priests not wanting to take some position I thought they should have, and I wasn't going to do the same thing to the Holy Father."

The two friends also traveled together to Africa, the ever widening field for missions and missionaries.

Throughout his life Samuel Stritch was destined to learn that on all the earth he had no lasting city. At this ceremony of farewell his clergy gathered about him, and the venerable Vicar-General, Monsignor O'Connell, rose to say: "It is a short nine years since our Boy Bishop came to Toledo. If his youthful appearance made us doubtful then, his brilliant mind soon convinced us. These nine years have been a great joy to the priests of the diocese." As though peering with prophetic eye into the future, the Vicar-General added: "There is no gift possible in the Church that we do not wish him. There is no gift he will not receive."

Mayor Jackson presided at the banquet. Dr. Stephen Mahon,

Methodist minister, Rabbi Michael Lichtenstein, and the Rev. Mr. McWilliams, Baptist pastor, were among the speakers. It is the type of tribute paid by these leaders of non-Catholic groups that gives a clear idea of the extent to which the personality of Samuel Stritch had unfolded, and of the quality of his leadership during this opening period of his episcopal career. Dr. Mahon, speaking for the non-Catholics of the city, said: "I want to express an appreciation of the spiritual quality Bishop Stritch has brought to Toledo. Those of you who followed him felt this religious pressure, but the rest of us have come to know the spiritual character of the man."

"For nine years," said Rabbi Lichtenstein, "he has been a blessing to our community and we surely shall miss him."

The Bishop replied that Toledo represented something so unique, so wonderful in his life that he gave up the burden of Toledo with regret. He made the comment that in his day he had observed the city throwing off the village psychology for a greater and wider culture.

Into the hearts of the silent throng facing him, he sent his farewell message: "Religion, education, and morality are the only safe supports for American democracy. Never before was God so necessary to man and to society as He is today. Unless the family life and home is sacred, society does not flourish. The greatest institutions of learning cannot produce teachers to equal good fathers and good mothers. . . . I leave you," he concluded, "but I take you with me in my heart."

With 400 persons from the Diocese of Toledo and the Archdiocese of Milwaukee, Bishop Stritch left his unfinished cathedral and boarded the special train for his new assignment. The great friend of his Toledo days, Msgr. Kinnane, ends an account of the Bishop's regime in the following manner:

"Here are the main points in his activity as the 'Boy Bishop,' as he called himself. But they do not show the outstanding characteristic of the man — the deep love he engendered in the hearts of all who were in touch with him, nor the deep love that he had for priests and people. . . . The picture that I keep of him in my study was taken just before his train pulled out for Milwaukee on November 18, 1930. He is trying to smile, but there is a pathos in his face that can bring tears."

VIII

QUIETLY, simply, as he had come to Toledo, with the same gracious smile — and the same empty pockets — Bishop Stritch steamed into Milwaukee on November 18, 1930. At an age far younger than is usual for a bishop when he is made an archbishop, when the depression of the 1930's lay like a heavy pall over the country, he was confronted with the problems and the augmented needs of an archdiocese that was to be a challenge to his administrative powers, to his charity, to his vision. It was a period that would put not only his courage, but his wisdom to the test.

The presence of Cardinal Mundelein, who came from Chicago to install the new Archbishop, contributed to the brilliance of the ceremony at St. John's Cathedral on Wednesday morning, November 19. Before leading him to the throne, the great Cardinal of the West in his eloquent way paid tribute not only to Archbishop Stritch's intellectual attainments and his administrative ability, but to his gentleness, patience, and consideration as evidenced in his ecclesiastical career. Standing at his throne, Archbishop Stritch gave his first message to his flock, pleading for a renaissance of Christian doctrine and practice, for union with the Church in combating the "dangerous theories of modern intellectual culture, based upon the shifting sands of humanism and naturalism."

On Wednesday, December 3, civic Milwaukee was warm with welcome. Governor Walter Kohler on behalf of the state of Wisconsin expressed a cordial tribute to the Archbishop. Mayor Hoan as well as other prominent citizens made addresses, and Dr. Potter, superintendent of public schools, characterized the Archbishop as the friend of children and a stout defender of popular education. "To this city," Dr. Potter continued, "composed of men of many creeds and political beliefs, his human qualities make a special appeal. Interpreter of the South to the North, and of America to Europe, he may become an interpreter of Milwaukee to the world. He brings promise of high civic accomplishment in the Archdiocese of Milwaukee."

Although Archbishop Stritch went far beyond being an interpreter of Milwaukee to the world, the words were intuitive in their evaluation of the type of service that his lifework would include: an interpreter for alien peoples, for divergent groups in the homeland, a builder of bridges, a destroyer of barriers. For this his earlier surroundings had fitted him. Although Irish by descent, he had begun life in a substantial neighborhood of Germans. He spoke the language and understood the mentality of Italy. He could read French, and though he knew only a little Polish, there were no confirmations he enjoyed more than those of Polish and Slovak children. His name, fortunately, satisfied the various language groups in Milwaukee. The Poles maintained that it was Polish, the Germans believed him a German, and the Irish knew that he was Irish. In consequence everyone was happy, and when the truth emerged they already loved him for himself and nationality made no difference.

The Archbishop was fully aware of the problems confronting him in those depressed and difficult years and was grateful for the spontaneity of the welcome accorded him. In his acknowledgment he sounded again the dominant chord of his thinking: the need for religion as "the only remedy for the social evils which today are threatening our world and our prosperity." While alluding to the changed conditions of living, thinking, and acting, as brought about by scientific inventions and discoveries, he added: "But even a greater thing than the changes caused by inventions and discoveries has come to pass. We have experienced the cataclysm of the World War, when thrones toppled, the map of more than a continent was remade, hatreds which we scarcely conceived as possible, were displayed. Human ideals were tarnished and we have scarcely yet assessed all the consequences. We live in a vortex of stupendous changes. No wonder many lost their mental balance, were unable to adjust themselves to conditions in the face of which the world was found almost impotent. . . . To many, I am their religious leader, their God-given shepherd. But to all, I hope, I shall always be ready to extend a helping hand; to unite in the preservation of our American liberties, which are forever safe only in the sacred embrace of religion. I thank you and I hope that the years God may give me to live, may be spent among you as a useful citizen, doing his share toward the realization of those ideals which make life worth while."

IX

IT WAS the First Friday of June. While Archbishop Stritch was learning the ways of his archdiocese and squaring his shoulders to its burdens, a young priest, not long out of the seminary and on his first assignment, received a mysterious call: "The Archbishop wishes to see you." As though an electric charge had been let loose, his nerves began to jump.

"Don't look so frightened, man," his pastor urged, with an understanding smile. The young priest's lips were dry. It was his first summons by the Archbishop.

"What can His Grace possibly want with me," he stammered, scarcely breathing.

"You must go at once and find out." The pastor was almost laughing now.

Young Father Atkielski walked quickly, examining his conscience on the way. What had he done amiss? What had he neglected to do? How would the Archbishop receive him? What answer should he give? He had not long to wait.

"Come in, Father," a friendly voice called. When invited to be seated the young priest ventured no farther than the edge of his chair. "And how is your pastor?" The southern accent sounded comforting in Milwaukee. "Does he treat you well? Are you overworked? Would you like a change? How would you like to be my secretary?"

The Archbishop sensed the young priest's fear. "You will soon be a better typist than I am, Father," he said with a reassuring smile. "I type with two fingers, you know; quickly, but not accurately. . . . And you must learn to drive; for we are going out to the lake in the old Nash Victoria."

The young priest was spellbound. Our Lord's words: "You have not chosen me. I have chosen you" seemed to dance paraphrased in the sunlight. "Can he mean it?" the young priest was asking himself while relief, wonderment, and hesitancy battled for supremacy within him.

The Archbishop did mean it, and he knew his man. This quick perception was the same special quality which enabled him in conversation, almost instantly when but a few words had been said, to grasp with a leap the total idea that a person might wish to convey. One of the greatest trials to his patience, therefore, was the individuals given to belaboring a conversation when he was miles ahead of it; for his thoughts came in conclusions in the intuitive way, and his snap judgments were the best.

Paradoxically, nevertheless, he was inclined to long deliberation and was a good listener. He has been known to sit in consultation with certain leaders of Catholic affairs, and listen quietly to their suggestions. Not at once, but perhaps a year or more later he would act upon those very suggestions. As his problems grew in complexity they drew more and more upon his own inward complexities; but to the world at large he remained simple, patient, gracious, and kind.

His early and complete dedication to his priesthood deepened, if possible, as he entered more vitally into the functions of an archbishop, loving the Church with ever growing intensity. That a bishop should always be available was his firm conviction. So accessible was he that many believed that they knew him well; but there were few who understood him truly: the nuances, the sensitivities of his finely strung temperament, the humility more profound than the natural simplicity, the asceticism hidden beneath the unfailing smile. We have the secretary's word for it that everybody knows him for what he did, that no one knows him for what he is.

In Milwaukee there was much ice to be broken. The Archbishop did it and with his own hands, so to say. Industrial difficulties played havoc on the south side of Milwaukee. The war had left ugly scars upon the various national groups. The groans of the poor sounded on all sides. Day and night the Archbishop suffered with them. Bravely he went into debt to carry on the works of charity.

The most tragic problem of all was the result of the defalcation of a local financial house that held many bonds of the poor parishes of the city. Although a number of these bonds were paid before they became due, the person who handled the money speculated with it and could not make good. When the matter grew into a public scandal he committed suicide. Silently the Archbishop took up this cross and met all the obligations, thus saving the credit of at least eighteen parishes, even though to do it forced him to make heavy loans on the part of the diocese.

In the meantime the St. Vincent de Paul Society, that right arm of relief, found itself burdened with a debt of $40,000. Again the Archbishop did not fail. He guaranteed the sum and ultimately paid it; but at the price of going begging for the love of Christ and His poor. His answer was prompt and effective: "If necessary," he said, "I shall go out with my tin cup."

X

"SISTER FREDERICKA, do please give Father Atkielski a cup of coffee and make him comfortable." The young secretary, newly arrived, heard the Archbishop's voice calling to the superior of the little group of Franciscan Sisters who were in charge of the episcopal household. Comfortable he was, as much as kindness could make him so; but the surprise of his new position, his inexperience, still lay like a weight upon his spirits.

The Archbishop knew this when he came over to his secretary's room on that first evening and settled down to smoke a cigarette with him. He knew also, with that unfailing intuition of his, that here was the man destined to be nearest to him, whom God had sent not only to work with him, but to share his living and thinking. This confidence soon manifested itself. In its warmth the younger man grew, until under the Archbishop's gentle training he caught fire from his leader and gave generously in return that which had been given to him. With his own robust individuality unimpaired, fearless in his judgments, he became the firm support of the Archbishop in dark and anguished hours. To him as perhaps to none other, Samuel Stritch revealed his inner self with all its complexities, its lights and shadows.

And shadows there were in that new life into which he had come. By nature inclined to moods of depression, there were days when the Archbishop would withdraw as it were, into an inner darkness. Later in his career, however, the outer evidences of moodiness had more or less vanished.

At any rate, regardless of personal tendencies, the Archbishop plunged positively and courageously into the many-sided work of his diocese. In the midst of economic stresses and vexatious external problems he did not lose hold of the inner situation, the care of his priests. He would write letters to them, perhaps six pages long, which left a powerful impression upon them. He suffered acutely when anything was amiss among them and when one or another slipped onto a wrong path he blamed himself. He blamed himself for everything and excused everything in others.

"Where did I make a mistake? In what have I failed?" In misery he would question his secretary. And all the priest in the youthful secretary would rise in comforting reassurance: "You haven't failed in anything."

"What makes them make such mistakes?" the Archbishop would say, musing sadly over some failure in discipline. "It is the human side. It is easy enough to see the bad side; but there is a good side which we shall never know. Never judge anybody, my boy, by the feathers. Francis de Sales was a gentleman to the nth degree; but he wore a hair shirt. Come, let us make the Holy Hour."

The keeping of the Holy Hour was a nightly custom. The Archbishop knelt in prayer, his secretary beside him. After the labors, the cares of the day came the quiet hour, the hour of peace before the Blessed Sacrament.

XI

IT WAS the day after Christmas. Only a few weeks after his civic reception the Archbishop came again to the Milwaukee Auditorium, but for an entirely different purpose. This time, after an official visit to the Jesuits, he occupied a box with the president of Marquette University and sat smiling while he watched the basketball game between Marquette and the University of Pittsburgh. In view of his past history in the field of sports, the news item: "Marquette University has a new and noted basketball fan," was keenly amusing. Had these enthusiasts never heard of the Horribles and the Terribles of North American College fame? He could still hear the voice of a classmate calling out: "That fellow can't catch a ball."

Perhaps the Archbishop could neither catch nor pitch a ball; but his interest went out to those who could. And it went much farther when he launched a powerful youth movement that was to gain such momentum during his regime that the C.Y.O. soon numbered 35,000 members in 275 parish units. With the future of the Church, of society, and of America in mind, and in concern for the building of a Christian character in the boys and girls, the young men and the young women of his flock, he provided new opportunities in education, in literature and the arts, in sports and hobbies. He left behind him a strong youthful army, the Christians and the citizens of a better tomorrow, because of his presence among them.

To achieve this end as well as to quicken the blood stream of his diocese into a new and forceful spiritual life, he drew the laity into collaboration with him, thus forming an apostolate of the faithful that meant Catholic Action in the sense that the Popes had envisioned it. Under his leadership the Holy Name Society gained vigor and rapidly increased in membership. The women also became organized for more efficient service. Ever mindful as a part of Catholic Action, of the possibilities inherent in a strong, diocesan paper, he unified the Catholic press of Milwaukee, with the present *Herald-Citizen* as a result.

Although in Toledo the Archbishop had built a central high school according to a concept extremely advanced for the time, he was, according to the opinion of some, not enthusiastic for Catholic high school education when he first came to Milwaukee. He appeared to believe that high schools and colleges should be limited largely to students of considerable ability who could make use of their education in life. Eventually, however, he changed his point of view and gave his support to expansion of Catholic high schools in the city.

During his years in Milwaukee the Archbishop was in friendliest relationship with the neighboring Archdiocese of Chicago. He came close to its spirit and won his way easily into the heart of its Cardinal, the extraordinary activities of whose career he watched with intense interest. On his frequent visits to Chicago he always saw Cardinal Mundelein and came into even closer association with him when he was made vice-chancellor of the Catholic Church Extension Society, that tremendous undertaking on the part of Chicago in aid of the Home Missions. This was the beginning also of his friendship with Archbishop O'Brien who was to be the loved companion of later years.

Rapidly the ties with Chicago were becoming more closely knit. In June of 1931 De Paul University conferred upon him the honorary degree of Doctor of Laws, and in the Chicago Civic Opera house he addressed 345 graduates of De Paul's Law, Commerce, and Liberal Arts colleges. As official ecclesiastical visitor to Quigley Seminary he became acquainted also with that flourishing preparatory training ground for priests of the Chicago diocese. Even the major seminaries of Chicago and Milwaukee were close neighbors. The relatively new and magnificent seminary of St. Mary's of the Lake at Mundelein, Illinois, is but a county away from the venerable St. Francis Seminary which, with the new Archbishop, celebrated its diamond jubilee in 1931.

Celebrations, however, were not the dominating events of the Archbishop's varied life, despite the fact that every year hundreds of children from the Catholic institutions of Milwaukee were his guests at a Christmas party in the staff room of St. Joseph's Hospital. Every little one received a present and a special smile as the long lines passed the Archbishop. In the state penitentiary at Waupun on a day in May the scene was totally different. For the first time, a Confirmation class had been formed in that institution and the Archbishop went to confirm twenty-four prisoners. In such diverse ways his busy days were spent.

XII

"ARE you coming with me?" The Archbishop asked with a mischievous smile, dropping casually into his secretary's room after their Holy Hour was over. "Next week I must be on my way with the tin cup. The poor are getting poorer, welfare funds are low, and we have a depleted St. Vincent de Paul Society. If I don't do it, I can't expect it of others."

"Am I coming with you? What a question!" The secretary had long ago fallen into the informality that the Archbishop wished from him. Differences of position were cast aside in this extraordinary friendship. It was man to man, sometimes father to son, but always friend to friend. The secretary, more than secretary, was even more than friend. He was home, a home to which the Archbishop loved to withdraw, where he could be most humanly himself. His secretary was the most effective remedy for the frequent loneliness of soul that was part of his nature.

"You have to be my conscience," he would say to Father Atkielski, "and if you see anything that needs correction you must tell me, whether it hurts or not." By the same token the Archbishop, and later the Cardinal, did not spare hurts to those whom he loved and whose perfection he desired above all else. He did not hesitate to say to his secretary: "You are too proud to admit your mistakes"; or at another time: "Look, son, you know me. Everything for your best interest. You can save your soul or lose it."

On the other hand he sensed the slightest trouble that concerned his friend. Whether it was illness in his family or any other difficulty, the question "Can I help?" was always immediate and he was ready at any moment to pray with him, perhaps the beads or the Divine Office. Strangely enough this deep affection engendered no partiality insofar as ecclesiastical preferment was concerned; nor did he ever as archbishop or later as cardinal heap favors upon those who were closest to him, whether of his immediate family or his clergy. Just as he once said: "Be a witness that I do not discuss politics," so in anything that savored of politics in ecclesiastical affairs he would have no part. There never was nor would be such a thing as a "Stritch man."

"How much money have I?" The Archbishop thrust his hands into his pockets; but there was no answering jingle. "You haven't any," the secretary replied with conviction. He was not uneasy however; for this was no new story. He had become thoroughly accustomed to the Archbishop's attitude toward money and was familiar with the slogan: "If you have two pennies, one belongs to the poor." Often the Archbishop did not keep even one of the proverbial two pennies for himself. Any beggar, old or young, deserving or undeserving, appealing or revolting, was Christ in disguise.

Year after year during a great part of his stay in Milwaukee, through nineteen counties the Archbishop traveled, preaching and asking alms in behalf of his poor. Whether it was to the Dells, to Green Lake, or to Ripon, no matter how many miles were covered, he always returned home for the night. Sometimes it was late and there were not many hours of sleep.

The air was growing gray one afternoon in winter. The snows lay heavy upon the empty fields and the wind blew a sharp whistle over the open countryside. Despite the sweater under his overcoat, the Archbishop was shivering. His southern blood always ran cold at the bite of the northern winter. With apprehension the secretary noticed his flushed cheeks, though his teeth were chattering, and implored him to return home and go to bed. The Archbishop would not hear of it. There was one town more to visit before the day was over for him. There was one more speech to make and he made it. A siege of pneumonia was the result; but the tin cup had fared well. The annual begging tours had produced $75,000 and the Archbishop was happy for his poor.

The secretary in the meantime had his troubles in keeping the Archbishop himself from looking like an object of charity. "I'm not going out with you like this," he would threaten. "Look at your shoes, your wrinkled clothes! After all, you are an archbishop and the disgrace would fall upon me for letting you go like that." The Archbishop did look, and smiled a mischievous smile while the secretary polished the shoes or sent them out for repairs and saw to it that the suit was pressed, often doing it himself. When the barber was finally summoned to administer a haircut, the secretary took a deep breath of relief.

It was not that the Archbishop in the least desired this type of service. He simply forgot all about himself. His mind was on larger and more disturbing issues, on needs other than his own, and the secretary lovingly took charge of the grooming. For his archbishop he would willingly be a tailor or a bootblack. Perhaps too he enjoyed the reversed relationship, for at such times, at least, the Archbishop was his child.

Absorbing as life was in Milwaukee, filled with work and many problems, the Archbishop did not forget the old friends in his former diocese. The following letter to a priest-friend, chaplain of a convent outside of Toledo, reveals a mood that came with the approach of spring when the prospect of a little rest lay invitingly in the offing: "My dear Father Joe,

"I was just thinking today about Ladyglenn. The first signs of spring must surely be about, and the weather fine. Just be sure to keep a bed for me, for I am coming to see you. When I get the spring engagements out of the way I am going to get a good rest with you. Maybe it will be warm enough to sit out at night and dream out loud. At any rate we shall go over in the garden and watch things grow. Pray for me every day. Love to the Sisters, 'Angels' and 'Kiddies.'"

XIII

FIVE years had passed since Archbishop Stritch came to Milwaukee. Thousands were gathered again in its auditorium, this time to celebrate with him the silver anniversary of his ordination. At an improvised altar he offered Pontifical High Mass. The dear friend and adviser of his boyhood, Bishop Morris of Little Rock, had come for the occasion, and the words of affection and paternal pride in his jubilee sermon stirred memories of forty years ago in Nashville, when Bishop Morris was young Father Morris and Samuel Stritch was his altar boy.

At a testimonial dinner in late April the clergy had anticipated the day by presenting him with a beautiful silver chalice. The evening of May 21, however, belonged to the laity who sponsored a concert with a sixty-piece symphony orchestra to accompany a chorus of 1500 children of the parochial schools, "these lambs of mine," as the Archbishop called them. He specially enjoyed choral singing and although he was never famous for his own singing, any more than for his penmanship, he had a theoretical knowledge of music for which he had once even received a gold medal. At any rate he was interested in music as he was in all the arts and saw to it that the Ward method was introduced into all the parochial schools of the diocese.

On July 7 the Archbishop received a further recognition of his anniversary at an enormous demonstration in Marquette Stadium when 30,000 members of the Holy Name Society received Holy Communion for him. In addition to these tributes of appreciation, the silver year brought an event that was filled with bright promise for the future. By his election as a member of the Administrative Board of the National Catholic Welfare Council, Archbishop Stritch was launched into activities destined to expand far beyond the limits of an archdiocese and eventually to assume a character not only national, but international.

This same year took him to Rome again, the first visit since his arrival in Milwaukee. He did not find "this poor old Pope" as Pius X had called himself on the unforgettable ordination day; but he did find another "dressed in white," another Pius, a veritable power house of Catholic Action, and Rome was always Rome. Like its ever flowing fountains, its inexhaustible spiritual mainsprings rise with a power that could renew the face of the earth, animate every freshet breaking forth in the hidden corners of the world, and fill it with the savor of the source.

Strong in the soul of Samuel Stritch was the feel of Rome. Here where Peter was, the Spirit breathed, the Spirit that could penetrate all the activities of men. It was this adherence to the source and the effort to translate the basic reality of Catholic truth into all the issues of life, that endowed Samuel Stritch with the dynamism which his gentle personality would not have led one to expect. Therefore every public invocation, every laying of a cornerstone, every speech at a banquet reached out beyond itself, because it carried the charge of a vital message.

"Discard God and you discard man," the Archbishop's words came at white heat when, in 1936, he blessed and laid the cornerstone of St. Robert's Church. "When men tear down churches, they do it not in the name of liberty, but in the name of tyranny. We are building this church that speaks of faith in God — to fix the foundation of real society. The commandment to 'love thy neighbor' is only the second part of that commandment calling upon man to love his God."

Many times while occupying the See of Milwaukee the Archbishop raised his voice concerning diverse problems: deploring the introduction of pagan principles into social welfare work, deprecating misrepresentations of the Vatican's position toward the Far East, decrying the persecution of the Jews. In clear terms he set forth the attitude of the Church with regard to gambling, stressed personal sanctification as the cure for modern social ills, called attention to the need for Home Missions, and cited the insistence of the Catholic Church upon charity as a continuous duty. On many other questions he gave clear directions to his people, and his pronouncements were attracting widespread attention and respect.

In a letter to Rabbi Joseph Baron of Milwaukee, the Archbishop gives the following expression to his position against anti-Semitism:

"In these times when nefarious propaganda is bringing untold sufferings to millions and stopping under specious pretenses the exercise of fundamental human right in many quarters, it is highly important that sane men keep cool heads. If there are certain individuals, who to gain and hold a popular audience, degrade themselves and abuse the trust reposed in them by misquoting, half-quoting and actually insinuating untruths, sane men, who know full well that in the end truth does conquer, must guide public opinion in safe channels.

"Now it is all too true that your people have been the victim in our day of a wicked movement which distorts truth and gilds falsehood. Against this wicked thing it is our duty to protest, for we claim to be the followers of Him Who proclaimed: 'I am the Truth.' Perhaps we entertain a more intimate sympathy with you these days, for Catholics, too, are the victims of vile propaganda and a very hatred of truth. The expression of our horror at the calumnies heaped on your people is natural; but I hope that all of us plumb this thing a little more deeply and discover for ourselves that at the bottom it is atheism. Defense is honorable, but in these times we should devote ourselves to the constructive task of bringing God back into the lives of men. Without Him there is no stable morality, no justice, no peace.

"You may be assured that I am always sympathetic to every effort to promote the universal recognition of human rights, which I hope we shall seek to found in God, without Whom they are but rhetoric."

XIV

IT WAS Christmas Eve, 1939. The Archbishop sat dressed in his robes as he had been while sitting for his portrait at Mount Mary College, and the bright smile still lingered in his eyes. The past year had swung heavily on its hinges, heavily and full of import. Early in its course the dynamic Pius XI had died and after the shortest conclave since 1623, Pius XII was reigning in his place. From the height of the papal throne he was bending all his forces in the struggle to bring peace to the world as he had done in his strenuous diplomatic years during and after World War I.

On this, his first Christmas Eve as Pope, in an eloquent allocution: *In Questo Giorno Di Santa* ("On this holy, happy day"), to which the attentive ear of the Archbishop of Milwaukee was sensitively attuned, His Holiness outlined the requisites for a just and honorable peace. In the silence of the approaching midnight hour Samuel Stritch reached out with all his being toward the Shepherd of all the world, with an intense desire in his own smaller sphere to help in this labor of love to all God's world. The recent expanding of his orbit of work would offer increased possibilities. At their last annual meeting in Washington, D. C., the archbishops and bishops of the United States had made him chairman of the Administrative Board of the National Catholic Welfare Conference.

One powerful leader had been taken from the ranks of the hierarchy. Suddenly, on October 2, the blow had struck: Cardinal Mundelein was dead, and the Archbishop lost both a neighbor and a friend. What a difference his absence would make! And the See of Chicago was still empty!

The clock was striking eleven. Before the last stroke the doorbell rang. The secretary jumped to his feet to answer the call. The Archbishop's eyes narrowed to instant alertness. Without a word the secretary handed him a yellow envelope, Western Union.

The Archbishop's face lost its joyous expression. It was a queer little habit of his, when in deep thought or when puzzled, to bring his finger up to the side of his nose. Those about him always recognized the sign. This time he took hold of the tip of his nose and sat motionless. Tensely, the secretary had his eyes fixed upon him. "I can't do it," he heard the Archbishop whisper, as though to himself. Then he knew. "You are going to Chicago!"

It was time to leave for the Cathedral. The Archbishop must say the Midnight Mass and the secretary serve as his master of ceremonies. Silently they went and in silence they returned. As yet the the Archbishop had disclosed nothing. "Why don't you let me be the first to congratulate you?" the secretary asked, trying to inject a little cheer into his voice when they were at home again. The Archbishop did not answer the question. "Just keep me company," he said instead. The minutes beat like hammers into the night while the clock ticked on.

"Can you be back at four?" the Archbishop asked on Christmas Day over the breakfast table. The secretary's hands were none too steady. He dropped his fork. "I'd much rather stay home," he said. "The family is expecting me; but I'll be back at four."

Upon his return, he found the Archbishop standing outdoors, waiting. "Let's take a drive," he suggested. This rather surprised the secretary. He had expected a brisk walk. The reason, however, soon revealed itself. "Let's go to Western Union," the Archbishop directed after they had driven a short distance. They drew up in front of the telegraph office. "You stay in the car," the Archbishop said when his companion jumped out to open the door. The secretary sat and waited.

In the meantime he was asking himself: "What can I do to distract him?" Clearly the Archbishop was suffering from a deep depression. His own heart was heavy with foreboding. A great change lay in the offing.

They passed the shop windows, desolate-looking things on Christmas Day. Through the plate glass, wax figures wearing ridiculous hats smirked at them. It was too absurd. The secretary burst into laughter: "Do look at those idiotic hats. And did you ever see such crazy shoes?" Ordinarily the Archbishop's sense of humor was quick as well as subtle; but today the shadows would not lift, even momentarily.

The telegram that he had sent was a plea to be spared the position offered him; but on the day after Christmas the answer came: It could not be done. They spoke of it freely now, the Archbishop and his secretary while they sat together at midnight. "You are going to Chicago," the secretary said gloomily. "I am sorry that our friendship is to end." "Don't be silly," was the Archbishop's quick reply. "Nothing will interfere with that."

"Tell me honestly," he begged before they parted for the night, "did I do good work here, so that I can say to my Maker: 'I accomplished what You asked of me, at least to the best of my ability'?" The old, self-accusing humility was at work again. Everything that had gone amiss was a reflection upon his inadequacy. He wanted no one to fail or even to falter. If it so happened, it was due to some shortcoming on his part. Once more the secretary had to be his conscience and the conscience reassured him.

He had many an injunction for Father Atkielski in the busy days that followed: "Be kind to this person. Be kind to that one. Look after so and so." Chicago, in the meantime, was astir. With its customary energy it sprang into the harness of enthusiastic preparation for the reception of its new Archbishop. Not only the civic authorities, but non-Catholic religious leaders shared this spirit. Already in early January a long roster of Protestant ministers gave united expressions of approval at the appointment of Archbishop Stritch.

In Milwaukee while the Archbishop was preparing to leave, the annual Catholic Charities drive was being launched, with a goal of $200,000. "The greatest gift you could give me," the Archbishop told his people, "would be the assurance that you have provided for Catholic Charities in the Milwaukee Archdiocese for another year." Wholeheartedly the archdiocese gave this assurance on Sunday evening, March 3, when 8000 thronged into the auditorium to bid the beloved Shepherd farewell, and one of the speakers presented to him the proceeds of the drive, a check for $210,667. On January 7, long before this official meeting, 5000 members of the Holy Name Society had on January 7 attended a rally at the auditorium to hear the Archbishop's farewell message: "Always walk with Christ and ever have Him as your model."

Although everyone was upset, an unusual silence had fallen upon the Archbishop's house. Sister Fredericka was busy about many things. She, with a little group of her Sisters, was going to Chicago to take charge of the new household. Nevertheless there were tears in her eyes. The secretary, as the day of departure drew nearer, avoided the Archbishop. On the day before his leaving, he bade him good-by, then withdrew again, keeping himself out of reach until the very last moment.

On Wednesday morning, March 6, at ten-fifteen, two trains carrying a delegation of clergy and laity left Chicago for Milwaukee. Bishop Sheil, administrator of the archdiocese, and Bishop O'Brien, Auxiliary Bishop of Chicago, headed the clergy, while Mayor Edward Kelly led the group of laymen which included some of the most prominent citizens of Chicago. A "Youth Special" train filled with high-school students who wished to pay fealty to the Archbishop at his house left at approximately the same time.

It was shortly after twelve o'clock when Bishop Sheil drove up to the Archbishop's residence. The house was astir; but the secretary was not in sight. The train was due to leave for Chicago at one o'clock. A throng of one thousand from Milwaukee waited at the station. The Archbishop was ready; but one more thing remained for him to do, the last and the hardest. He ran up to the second floor. "Romy," he called, "O Romy!" A dejected figure emerged. The secretary made a brave effort to smile. The rest of the story he himself tells: "I fell apart."

XV

IT WAS two-thirty p.m. and while the train from Milwaukee pulled into Chicago, the Union Station fairly rocked with greetings of welcome from a mass group of 50,000, including 20,000 youths and children of the C.Y.O. who, under their director, Bishop Sheil, were taking a leading part in the ceremonies of reception. From a platform specially erected, Bishop Sheil presented to this great audience a slight gray-haired man with a warm, contagious smile who, when he began to speak, drew his hearers with immediate appeal. The music of twelve bands with a chorus of 500 voices echoed through the vast station until the parade formed that was to escort the Archbishop to the Cathedral, and then on to his new home.

The Archbishop had, of course, been in Chicago many times. How different was its aspect now while driving up North State Street to the Cathedral of the Holy Name where Cardinal Mundelein's empty throne was standing in wait! From there the procession continued up State Street to its end at Lincoln Park where, at the corner of North Avenue, the stately Victorian house of many chimneys stands, aloof from the traffic, among its tall and ancient trees. Papal and American flags, ecclesiastical symbols, the Archbishop's coat of arms with their flashes of color brightened the somber brick walls with an air of festivity. The heavy door had swung wide open, the formal and canonical induction took place immediately as the Administrator and the consultors turned over to the new Archbishop the administration of the largest archdiocese in the United States.

In humble obedience Samuel Stritch bent his back to this burden. When recalling Toledo he had said: "God must be good to me. I was only a boy when He gave me this terrible responsibility." He was no longer a boy, though still the youngest of archbishops; but responsibilities had grown apace and in keeping with his years the burdens had increased.

Once more he was made to feel that he had no lasting city. Once more he was made to see that it was not his destiny to settle quietly into the permanence of accustomed tasks. Progressively, up to now, his work had gained in momentum. The whitening harvest was spreading over expanding fields. Would Chicago be the end of the journey? Would this be the last long stop on the way to eternity?

The wind blew fresh from off the lake on the morning of March 7. It was the feast of St. Thomas Aquinas and the day had been specially chosen in honor of the Patron of Catholic Education. For three hours a crowd had waited for the procession to the Cathedral which was scheduled to begin at ten o'clock in preparation for the Solemn Pontifical Mass at ten-thirty, at which Bishop Griffin of Springfield, Illinois, the Archbishop's classmate of Roman days, officiated.

Almost the entire hierarchy of the United States was present, as well as representatives from Canada and Mexico, churchmen of all degrees, members of religious orders, and as many of the laity as the church could hold. The Archbishop's family occupied the front pews. The mayor of Chicago was there, as well as many other prominent citizens. In fact, the civic enthusiasm gave evidence of the realization that, aside from religion, Archbishop Stritch was welcomed as a valuable asset to the development of the city.

The Most Rev. Amleto Giovanni Cicognani, apostolic delegate to the United States, performed the ceremony of installation and in his sermon paid tribute to the Archbishop's priestly career, to his activities in the fields of charity, catechetical instruction, education, and labor.

"Your new Shepherd," he said, "brings with him nothing material or earthly, neither wealth nor the splendor of earthly glory. He comes with a paternal heart, with the qualifications of a pastor, with the program of an apostle. . . . The new Archbishop is here with you, in the Name of the Lord. . . ."

When the Archbishop mounted the pulpit, his inaugural address carried his ever urgent message, a plea to the clergy and the people to fight the force of materialism by a return to God.

"In my poor person," he said, "you see the Shepherd whom Pius has sent. I come among you as Christ's ambassador. . . . If I must command, then let my words be those of the ambassador of Christ and not of a master. If I must reprove, then let it be to seek out and help a soul and not to secure mere conformance.

"Together we shall walk with Christ and try to love Him more and more and let men see the peace and the joy of Christ in our souls. . . . Today we dedicate this beginning to our Blessed Lady, the Queen of Apostles, and we beg her to intercede for us with her Divine Son, that our days in Chicago, be they long or short, may be filled with works for God's Church."

At the dinner given for the visiting dignitaries and the diocesan priests at the Drake Hotel, the Apostolic Delegate, replying to the toast to the Pope, paid Archbishop Stritch the surpassing compliment of finding in him points of resemblance to the Holy Father, especially in his "complete sacrifice of self to the work of the Church, the total disappearance of personal interests in order that a God-given mission may be fulfilled."

In conclusion the Delegate referred to the great desires in the heart of Pius XII for "universal peace, harmony of nations, and the widespread propagation of the faith and of the charity of Christ."

On this opening day of the life of Samuel Stritch as Archbishop of Chicago, these words: "Universal peace, harmony of nations, propagation of the faith . . ." have a prophetic sound. Quietly he must have absorbed them, the echoes of that which lay germinating in his own heart. Three days later, on March 10, at a reception in the Chicago Stadium, attended by representatives of the 421 parishes, the new Archbishop was formally presented to his large spiritual family.

Milwaukee with its dire needs during the depressed 1930's had served as a training ground for the tremendous problems that confronted him in Chicago. He saw at once the necessity of expanding all the resources of the archdiocese and heavily they drew upon his own resources, his quick understanding, his answering interests, his utter dedication and priestliness. Against the tensions from without, he needed also the balancing power of an inner force, something perhaps closely akin to sanctity, a love diffusive of itself and linked with a grace of manner that would find its way to people in all their diversity and encourage them to find their way to him. According to his interpretation a bishop was not a symbol; he was the heart of his diocese.

With consummate skill he selected those most fitted for the positions that he had to man, those upon whom he could depend for the smooth functioning of a large archdiocese, its mechanics so to say. It was also his way of administration, that when he found the right person for a given work, he charged him with full responsibility for it, trusted him completely, and did not interfere with him. This policy left him more free to deal directly with the people, to make himself accessible to them, never to refuse to do anything that was asked of him, if humanly possible. It gave him free range also to inaugurate or to increase momentums in the multiple directions of human relations: matters of Christian social living, labor and interracial problems, education in all its phases. It would leave him free to build bridges from diocesan and civic, to national life, from national to international life, to facilitate the functioning of a Church militant, fully accoutered, in the achieving of its objective: the circulation of health-giving life through the Mystical Body of Christ.

It was pre-eminently through their association in the work of Church Extension, to which Bishop O'Brien had devoted the greater part of his life, that Archbishop Stritch found this dear companion whose cheerfulness and ready wit brightened the way over many a thorny path. Since he was the Junior Auxiliary, Archbishop Stritch, although younger, playfully called him Junior, which name later diminished into the affectionate title of "Juny." They were together on many a journey, especially in later years. Sometimes it was to Rome, at other times to Hobe Sound in Florida, where Cardinal Mundelein had bought a winter diocesan home.

"What's new in Florida?" a returning priest was asked on one of these occasions.

"The Boss is playing golf."

"How is his game?"

"Like you would expect it to be."

Bishop O'Brien, however, settled the question for all time.

"It was perfect," he said. "Perfection, according to the dictionary, is that which cannot be improved."

Looking ahead to the future of his archdiocese, Cardinal Mundelein once expressed the conviction that his successor would be a prelate of great learning, great piety, and great personal sanctity. Through Divine Providence the groundwork was laid. With such a well-prepared field awaiting, a saintly and scholarly archbishop needed to consolidate the gains and to bring greater honor and glory to God and His Church.

The *New World* has told the sequel, saying that Archbishop Stritch comes, not as a theorist, but as an administrator with experience, and not as a stranger. He had become familiar long ago with the problems of education, he was at home in missionary endeavor, additionally so after his appointment as vice-chancellor of the Church Extension Society. In Milwaukee he had already perfected a youth program, and had dealt with numerous racial and language groups. There too he had been the champion of the Catholic press and was brilliantly successful in making of the *Herald-Citizen* a strong diocesan paper.

It is not surprising, therefore, that within a week of his arrival, the Archbishop turned his attention to an apostolate of the press in Chicago. With the belief that the diary of a diocese is its newspaper, he set himself to the task of building up his archdiocesan paper, the *New World*.

For this purpose he launched a student crusade and whipped up the fervor of priests, sisters, and school children in support of the project. Happily, nearly everyone had seen him and he spared no personal energy in going through the city outlining districts for rallying points. Mercy High School was the scene of an enormous rally, so successful that one of the staff of the *New World* in presenting the Archbishop forgot everything but his own enthusiasm, and, with the intention of paying tribute to his extraordinary personal efforts, called him the Number One newsboy of the diocese, the best salesman in Chicago. In consternation, when he realized what he had said, he went to the Archbishop, protesting that he had blundered terribly, but had meant no disrespect. "Not at all," the Archbishop replied. "Why not? So long as it sells the *New World*."

From 10,000 paid subscribers in 1940 the list mounted to 147,000 in 1950 and later to 210,000, probably the largest circulation of any diocesan newspaper in the world. Obviously, the Archbishop is not responsible for all that appears in his diocesan paper; but it is important as a medium through which he can speak to his people as their Shepherd. His attitude toward the press was in keeping with one of the ideals of St. Pius X who had said: "In vain will you build churches and schools unless at the same time you wield the offensive and the defensive weapons of the Press." Therefore the progress of the *New World* was a source of joy, and in vision the Archbishop looked forward to a Catholic Sunday newspaper of the future.

XVI

IF THE chancery of the Archdiocese of Chicago is one of the busiest of ecclesiastical crossroads, the quiet, old-fashioned building painted gray, gives no sign of it. If its Archbishop between the years 1940 to 1958 was the dynamic center of a thousand projects, the gentle Father in the purple-bound cassock did not reveal it while he sat at his desk on the second floor, receiving visitors with a smile of welcome, placing himself at the disposal of each, quite as though he were there for him alone.

He was becoming acquainted with his diocese in its individual features as well as in its extensive total aspects, a tremendous power geared for action that he must stimulate and direct to further functioning. That which he had begun in Toledo and accomplished in Milwaukee must be fitted to the measure of Chicago. And yet there must be no Procrustean bed. Chicago must be interpreted in terms of itself. Every city has its own especial character and cannot be stamped with the individuating marks, even of a neighbor city. Happily it was part of the natural equipment of Samuel Stritch to grow into the atmosphere of the place that was allotted to him, so that he soon became a part of it, and it in turn became a part of him.

Chicago with its energetic temperament, its native enthusiasm, took him at once into its great bustling heart and helped to arouse the nation to an increasing awareness of his influence as a Christian leader. According to the testimony of those associated with him, the Archbishop had also the quality of inspiring an almost fierce loyalty in those who worked under his direction. Both priests and laity loved him. Perhaps this was but an inevitable response to his attitude toward both. Always primarily the priest, he respected this dignity in every other priest and was therefore intensely loyal to him. He was never harsh to his priests, never faultfinding. He encouraged no priest to resign; but always found a way of letting him be useful. When a priest made some mistake, the Archbishop suffered the agony of it and spared nothing in providing for his protection and rehabilitation.

One day a shamefaced priest appeared at the chancery and sat waiting in the anteroom of the Archbishop's office. He had nothing to expect but a severe reprimand and perhaps a drastic punishment. The door opened. Dejectedly he rose to meet his verdict; but the Archbishop's hand was extended. "I knew," he said, "that you would find your way back to the love of God."

It was these tragic possibilities in human nature that gave poignancy to his joy when row upon row of young levites knelt before him in the sanctuary and he bestowed upon them, one after another, each separate power of the priesthood. Looking upon them in their youthful fervor, many were the times that his solicitude prompted him to say: "I would give my right arm if they would always remain as they are now when I ordain them."

To lay projects the Archbishop gave complete freedom and encouragement, so that the laity felt themselves called upon to play a vital part in the affairs of the diocese and enabled thereby to contribute to the Catholic Action of the world. The Archbishop opened all the windows of his diocese. Priests and people worked together. Activities already in progress or newly undertaken entered upon a period of fulsome flowering. Since a solid intellectual formation was a necessary basis for lay activity, Chicago placed emphasis upon a study of the liturgy, Scripture, the papal encyclicals, the social doctrines of the Church for the purpose of embodying all these forces into daily living.

Lively little groups met in bookshops, apartments, classrooms, sometimes in restaurants. University professors met with journalists, workers, students, and seminarians, with priests and nuns. Many influences, notably the Interracial Council and the Cana Conference, emerged from the study week ends at Childerly in the suburban area of Chicago, where the Calvert or Newman Club of the University of Chicago maintains a lay retreat house.

Other phases of this spiritual revival found expression in the Adult Education courses, the Christian Family Movement, in the impetus given to organizations such as the Young Christian Workers and the Young Christian Students. The head chaplain of the three specialized lay movements mentioned above, the Y.C.W., Y.C.S., and the C.F.M., was appointed, in addition, to work with the diocesan clergy in spreading Catholic Action on a parish level. Chicago was the first diocese in which a priest was assigned to this particular task.

Behind it all was the Archbishop, a highly geared listener, never saying "No" to a creative idea, always willing to think about it or to permit it to be given a try. "It is not enough," he said, "to go to the Sacraments and attend Sunday Mass. We must live and participate in the life of the Church. What we are trying to do is to educate people to understand what it means to be a Catholic."

His own motivation in allowing this latitude to the development of new apostolic techniques becomes apparent in his words: "These days there opens to us a great opportunity. If the tragedies of the time are carefully analyzed, it will be found that at the core of them are moral and religious problems. To present to men the Christ and to cry to them, 'Behold your King' is our mission and opportunity. With God's help and the support of a devoted clergy and a loyal laity, we shall try our utmost to be true to our sacred office and be an unflinching witness of the Saviour."

XVII

"IT IS still early," the Archbishop's Chicago secretary said after dinner one evening when the days were growing longer and the premonitory softness of spring was in the air. "Shall we go for a drive?" "That would be pleasant," the Archbishop replied. He never requested a drive; but when his secretary made the offer he accepted gladly when he happened to be free.

The secretary quite naturally expected to swing over to Lake Shore Drive and up through the lovely northern suburbs; but the Archbishop had a different idea. "Let us go through the South Side or over to Maxwell Street," he suggested. The South Side as he meant it was the populous Black Belt so called, where the Negroes lived. Maxwell Street lay in the congested Jewish section of the West Side. It was alive with a babel of voices, buying, selling, bargaining, clamoring for attention. The wagons of venders crowded the street and all the men, women, and children of the neighborhood seemed to have gravitated to its sidewalks.

The Archbishop looked and listened. Regardless of color or race, people were of deep concern to him. He wanted to know this great, teeming city to which he had been sent.

During a visit to one of the hospitals one day, the Archbishop stopped at the bedside of an old Negro, who told him that he was a Baptist preacher. "Where are you all from?" the Archbishop asked in the dear vernacular of the South. The Negro's eyes glowed. "From Tinnesee, Reverend; from Cleveland, Tinnesee." It was the Archbishop's turn to be surprised and a warm, reminiscent light leaped into his eyes. Cleveland! The poor little corner to which, with missionary longing, he had so wanted to go when he was a very young priest.

His missionary inclinations, however, had a certain degree of fulfillment when, as Archbishop of Chicago, he became also the chancellor of the Church Extension Society. In 1941 at a general meeting in Washington he was appointed head of the American Board of Catholic Missions which was instituted in 1937 by the bishops of the United States. For the bishops working in the Home Mission fields he had words of enthusiastic praise. "Now the Church is actually growing on these missions," he said, "and some of the finest work done by us in the United States is done by the Bishops for the Home Missions. . . . In these times we must be ready to meet emergencies. . . . There must be careful planning and funds must be made available for doing a large work in the field of education and social centers. The mere building of chapels will not suffice."

It is an interesting sidelight on the many-faceted character of Archbishop Stritch to hear him speak about a "substantial reserve" and "funds available" when it was often uncertain as to whether or not he had a dime in his pocket. Under the law of Illinois the Archdiocese of Chicago is a corporation sole, of which the Archbishop is the one member. Millions of dollars pass through his hands. Of these, Samuel Stritch, Archbishop of Chicago, was careful to the penny; while Samuel Stritch the person, on a journey for instance, might have to ask his secretary: "Have you any money? I want to tip the porter."

A close associate, commenting on the Archbishop as a rare mixture of tough-minded practicality and unworldly piety, once said: "If I were doing his job for the money, I wouldn't take 10,000 bucks a week." It was said of Cardinal Mundelein that he would have made an excellent banker. In reference to this accepted fact a Catholic bank official admitted with evident amusement that Archbishop Stritch came into the bank apparently with no such qualifications and they gave him three times as much.

He was not domineering with his staff. Perhaps that is why they affectionately called him "The Boss." With all these things going on about him, it is well if we wish to know him as he was from within, to let his own words reveal him: "Throughout my activities the thing uppermost in my experience is the tangible presence of God."

Both the piety and the practicality alluded to, served well in the cause of the missions. In the introduction to one of the reports of the Extension Society the Archbishop wrote: "The Board . . . has chosen the Spanish-speaking Catholics of the Southwest and the Negro missions of the South for special consideration, because these two groups are the outstanding mission interests of the Church in the United States. . . . Out of all this there is coming a great harvest of souls."

In this as in other charities the Archbishop's interest began at home, but did not remain there. He reached out to the Philippines, the Bahamas, to Puerto Rico, Guam, and the Canal Zone. Though the Bahamas belong to Great Britain, he considered it a privilege to help them and was grateful to the Holy See for the permission to do so. He asked that these mission needs be kept constantly before the minds of priests and people as a participation in the Apostolate of the Church in helping our spiritually underprivileged brothers. "Without an interest in the missions," said the Archbishop, "our Catholic life would not be normal and full."

XVIII

"IT'S good to be home," said the Archbishop, with a smile at his secretary across the table. It was not part of Monsignor Fitzgerald's duties to be present at dinner every evening; but nothing that was not mandatory could keep him away. He delighted in the Archbishop's conversation, his wealth of information, his wide variety of interests, his agility at repartee. History was his great treasure chest, and one could entice him at will into remembering its most hidden recesses.

The time-worn dictum that no man is a hero to his valet went completely into reverse when applied to the Archbishop and his various secretaries. The friend and companion of Milwaukee, that other self of his, never wavered in his devotion. Every day he telephoned. Every Saturday he came to Chicago, and the old relationship continued according to its former pattern.

The Archbishop was now thoroughly settled in what he called "the quietest house in the city." Sister Fredericka and her little community who lived as in a convent on the remote third floor, kept the wheels of home free from all friction. Trixie, the toy Boston bull, was the court jester, following the Archbishop about, climbing up to his shoulder when he sat at his typewriter, or walking into the reception room to make a critical inspection when there were visitors, and leaving it with dignity when the Archbishop said: "Trixie, you may go."

The canary upstairs in the Archbishop's study was another favorite who helped to make the house a home, and with whom the Archbishop had intimate little conversations. The large and beautiful upper room of many windows, looking out upon the trees, held many things that the Archbishop loved. Row upon row of well-filled bookshelves lined the wall, for he was still an inveterate reader. His mother's picture hung in a special corner above a chair where he would sit to say his office, and St. Pius X — then Blessed — his unforgettable ideal, stood in full figure upon his desk. Perhaps more than once after a harassed day, the Archbishop thought of what he himself had related of St. Pius X, that this loved Pope used to go into his private chapel at the end of a long, difficult day, kneel, look at the Tabernacle, and say: "Lord, I've done the best I could. Now it's up to You to take care of the Church."

A number of friends of the other world adorned the adjoining bedroom. A picture of the Boy Jesus was there, the youthful Samuel, Mother Cabrini, St. Therese of Lisieux, and on a bedside table a golden reliquary with a relic of St. Anthony Mary Claret, after the latter's relatively recent canonization. Prominent near the windows stood a handsome carving of our Lady with a *prie-dieu* before her. This place was for the final night prayers, the closing act of the day.

In these surroundings everything was in order, everything breathed of peace, but beyond the quiet house a storm was brewing, and the world was filled with grim foreboding. The Archbishop had already taken part in every preventive measure that was in his power. In 1940 he was chairman of the committee which signed a joint pastoral on social justice issued by the bishops of the United States. The call of the bishops carried the voice of Pius XII: "Bring God back into Government!" Our economic life needed reorganization and they were sounding the alarm.

On September 20, 1941, the Archbishop dedicated a National Catholic Community Service Club at 1122 South Wabash Avenue, Chicago. On September 22 of the same year the Archbishop was in Springfield addressing a mass meeting of the Midwest Regional Conference of the N.C.W.C., having as its theme: "Faith and Service — For God and Country." In his speech the Archbishop told the delegates that the greatest opportunities since the breakdown of the Empire of the West face this Christian generation.

Then, like a sudden doom the lightnings of Pearl Harbor leaped into the sky and the world shook with oncoming thunder. Just before the Japanese attack the tireless American bishops had formed a special committee, with Archbishop Stritch as chairman, to promote the Pope's Peace Plan. Although this committee, after the hideous interruption, was to be reorganized in a later year, and the Archbishop's forces had to spend themselves during the interval in the global charity of war relief, he nevertheless forged ahead in his thinking and looked constructively into the ominous future. "It is necessary for us," he said, "to give thought to the winning of the peace as it is necessary to make every sacrifice for the winning of the war."

The Archbishop, so reticent about his personal politics, was fearless and outspoken when it concerned affairs of national and international import, and when Christian principles were at stake. He avoided dramatics at all times; but when something had to be done, he did it. He never forgot, during the years of war, that as chairman of the Bishops' Committee on the Pope's Peace Points, his was the responsibility of interpreting accurately the Holy Father's constructive thinking on a matter concerning the welfare of the whole human race.

In an article for *Extension* magazine, March 22, 1943, the Archbishop not only pointed out the principles of a Christian peace, but emphasized the duty of everyone to work for their accomplishment. "When we talk of a new postwar world," he wrote, "we should be talking of the interpretation of new problems and conditions in the light of our inherited culture and not of any sort of substitution of a new culture."

The Archbishop quoted fully the five points in question which, as he said, will unfold the picture in large detail of a world in which our culture can grow and flourish. "Our culture is a family-society," he wrote in conclusion. "The rights and dignity and sanctity of the family are imbedded in it. . . . The rights of the family are so intimately related to the economic rights of man that the defense of the family is a postulate for the recognition of sane economic demands of individuals and property. In vain will you fight for our freedoms against the aggression of the totalitarian States and militaristic Japan if you suffer little minds, alien to our culture, to do injury to the families of our nation. The peace crusader, in his undertaking to defend human rights and human dignity and give them wider reaches, must encompass in his aims the social emancipation of the family."

On November 8, 1943, the five peace points as given by Archbishop Stritch appeared in the magazine *Life*. Their outline is included in the following quotation: "Justice, not vengeance, must dictate our attitude towards the vanquished, and where justice falls short, enlightened charity must be the guide." The second point calls for the deliverance of nations from the burden of large armaments. The third point suggests an "association of nations which will make the peace treaty a living, workable thing." The fourth point says: "Peacemakers must search out diligently the needs of each nation, carefully evaluate them and earnestly try to satisfy them." The fifth and final point declares: "Religion alone can give life, authority, and binding force to human law and international agreements."

XIX

CHICAGO was sweltering. The day had been breathless with midsummer heat and even the early evening brought no breeze. Along North Avenue the people from farther west were streaming toward the lake. To some of the venturesome ones the grass around the quiet house on the corner of North State looked invitingly green. An invasion followed and before long the lawn was strewn with children and their panting mothers.

No prohibitive sound came from the house with the many chimneys and the clamor grew apace. It had reached its height when Mayor Kelly passed, taking his evening walk. Irate at this audacity, he rang the Archbishop's bell and expressed his regret at the disturbance. "What disturbance?" the Archbishop asked, with his disarming smile. "I shall send the police immediately," the Mayor retorted, "and tell them to see that this never happens again." "No, indeed," said the Archbishop, "these too are my people. They are hot and it is cooler here. They are welcome to stop and enjoy the grounds."

More and more the Archbishop, lenient and accessible toward every need at home, expanded his interests to the needs of the world. For him the year 1943 palpitated with significance. At the meeting in December, 1941, of the Bishop's Committee for the Pope's Peace Points, of which Archbishop Stritch was chairman, Father Harry C. Koenig, the librarian of the major seminary of the Chicago Archdiocese, St. Mary of the Lake at Mundelein, was invited to compile a book on the Pope's Peace Programs.

A reliable basis for such an undertaking was available in a French book compiled by Yves de l'Abrière who in Paris was associated with the Jesuit magazine, *L'Etude*, and later became the official representative for the Holy See at the League of Nations. Archbishop Stritch, at work with the Catholic Association for International Peace, made every effort to popularize the Papal Program for Peace and promoted with all his enthusiasm this book of 900 pages which, under the auspices of the American hierarchy, appeared in May, 1943.

And at an April meeting in Washington the bishops had come to grips with a problem of the moment. The war was in full progress. Something must be done, they decided, for the victims of the war. Archbishop Stritch threw the fullness of his ability into it and became largely instrumental in setting up the Catholic War

Relief as an organization, in the June of 1943, with Archbishop Mooney of Detroit as chairman.

From November to November in 1945 and 1946, Archbishop Stritch was chairman of Catholic War Relief. He understood at close range the respective problems of Poles, Lithuanians, and Hungarians, largely the groups belonging to his archdiocese, and in Chicago he resolutely pushed programs for displaced populations. As for Italy, his knowledge of the situation was complete. Accurately and without hesitation he was able to cite the details of Italian economy to the American Committee on Italian Emigration. To each national group he gave his entire mind as though he belonged exclusively to each.

This efficiency, together with that of his associates, had its results. The Catholic War Relief grew into the largest single volunteer relief agency. Based on its plan of action, 110 million dollars' worth of relief goods found their way into fifty-four countries.

Archbishop Stritch not only interpreted and disseminated an international program of peace, but contributed directly to one of its essentials. It was said of him: "This man lives what he believes." He believed in teaching and preaching to the world the conditions of a true and lasting peace; but he believed also in providing the material help that belongs to the foundations of peace; for starving people are not inclined toward peace.

Not only was Archbishop Stritch in his labors for peace the Pope's faithful messenger; but his charity and manner of action had the universal quality that belonged to Pius XII. Instinctively he thought and felt with the Church on every occasion.

XX

"WHEN are the Slovaks having their parade?" the Archbishop asked his Vicar-General while getting ready to leave the chancery after a crowded morning. "Next Sunday, Your Excellency," Monsignor Casey replied. "But you are having Pontifical High Mass at the Cathedral at ten o'clock and a Confirmation at four. You can't make it."

"O yes I can," the Archbishop said with conviction. "I can work it in at two o'clock." "You will kill yourself," the Vicar-General exclaimed. "Yes," said the Archbishop in his leisurely way, "I suppose it does cost a lot to bury archbishops."

The Vicar-General had no further reply. He had noticed that after these first three or four years the Archbishop was, if possible, becoming increasingly available. He accepted any and every engagement that it was humanly possible to fulfill. Whenever he could, he administered Confirmation himself. "It is my ecclesiastical golf," he replied when his priests remonstrated with him.

He dreaded the day of the desk priest, for to him it was necessity to express himself in activity, and he believed it his mission as Shepherd to be among the people. Despite this inner urge his manner was always calm. He never bustled and never shouted.

On one stormy day however, he broke all records. Something had gone inexcusably, exasperatingly wrong. What would the Archbishop do? Those about him waited, breathless. This certainly warranted an explosion, a thunderous shout that would make the rafters tremble. The Archbishop did not speak; but a pencil went flying across the room and no one ever forgot it.

Everyone who knows Chicago has at least heard of its famous stockyards. Behind them human beings live. They represent many faiths, although 95 per cent of the district is Catholic. The Archbishop did not forget this remote, congested section. On March 21, 1944, he sent his personal check of $500 to the director of the Back of the Yards Council, whose work has attracted nationwide attention. "The Back of the Yards Neighborhood Council," he wrote, "representing more than 185 community organizations of the stockyards' district, has rendered educational, domestic, medical, and social advantages to hundreds of families in this thickly populated Chicago industrial district." The gift, he said, was a small token of his appreciation of the good work that the Council is doing.

Only a few days later we find him absorbed in quite a different topic. While speaking at the fifth annual Catholic high school music festival in which more than 1000 students participated, the Archbishop assailed "music which is inspired by dirty commercials, that music which has no regard for lifting a man up and making him live with the beautiful and good — that music which teaches a man that reason and free will are not important to his career." He further pointed out that the "right kind of music can send boys and girls into the world with a love for the beautiful, scorning the music of the primitive, which degrades and lowers a man, making him forget that he is a man."

Civic affairs also made their demands upon the Archbishop. On the afternoon of May 23 he delivered the invocation at a celebration with an interesting name: "I Am an American Day." His invocations were never a formula and he found them adaptable instruments for carrying a message. Happily for the numerous calls that came to him, he was a gifted extemporaneous speaker. "Could we get the manuscript?" newspapermen would ask the secretary, and the frequent answer was: "I don't think he'll have one."

When he did provide a manuscript he would dictate the speech in the same extempore way at which his amanuensis never failed to marvel. Usually his spontaneous talks or sermons were of a quality superior to those that he worked over. He took seriously the obligation of a bishop to be a teacher and to preach "in season and out of season." On one such occasion, having apparently taken no time to prepare, his secretary asked: "Are you going to have a manuscript?" "No," said the Archbishop, "I'll think up something on the way driving down." Owing to his constant reading habit and wide background of historical knowledge, he could reach back into his mind at any moment, quote at will, and build his own thinking into a form that would appeal to his audiences.

It was in 1944 that the Archbishop wrote a series of articles for the *Chicago Sun*, entitled "Pattern for Peace," in which he advocated an international juridical institution "with full authority to settle disputes on the interpretation of international law." To this he related his favorite theme of charity. "Justice," he said, "if we embrace it, can remove all hindrances to peace. But peacemaking is the work of love."

Christmas came in 1944, still under the clouds of war. The Catholic War Relief was doing its utmost and the Archbishop's heart was in it; but he did not forget the 100 underprivileged little chaps from 50 of the poorer parishes of Chicago, for whom he played Santa Claus by keeping up the tradition of clothing them with complete outfits from overcoats to socks and ties. Every year at Christmas time a new group gathered in the Cathedral Grammar School, were taken to one of the big stores in the Chicago Loop, and after making their selections the noisy, happy throng were the Archbishop's guests at a turkey luncheon in the restaurant of the store.

Peace had not yet come at Easter time, in 1945. The Archbishop grieved with the Gold Star Mothers and directed his Easter message especially to them. With them he wished to pray that the leaders of nations "see to it that the thing these boys died for be realized, that the Peace of Easter come to men and nations."

XXI

THE flags of many nations were flying over San Francisco in the year 1945 and a weary-eyed world was looking hopefully toward the City of Saint Francis. Among the throng that walked its precipitous streets and breathed the invigorating air of the Pacific, was one who was listening with all his soul for the first faint strains of peace. He was an emissary. Someone at home was waiting. The report must be not only accurate, but complete. Therefore in all those many-worded sessions, the secretary of Archbishop Stritch, who knew his jurisprudence well, let nothing escape him.

Not long afterward, on July 13, the Archbishop expressed some of his reactions in a sermon at the Pontifical Mass in the Slavo-Byzantine rite celebrated at the Cathedral of Chicago in honor of Slav Church Unity Day.

"Allowing for certain undeniable defects," he said, "the San Francisco Charter remains the only promise the world has that international anarchy will not be permitted to return.

"The people of the United States must assume responsibility in international affairs and repudiate the traditions of political and economic isolationism. America must participate in an international organization.

"We assumed a great responsibility when we went into the war. We have broken with our past tradition of isolationism and we have done so rightly. We are the most powerful nation in the world, but by that very fact we have much to give the world and an obligation to do so."

He emphasized the fact that while there are imperfections in the

San Francisco Charter, "much of what the Conference accomplished was undeniably good, and the deficiencies in the Charter's framework can be eliminated so that the rights of all nations, regardless of size or race, can be respected. At least in principle, the days when great nations could victimize the small nations are gone. . . ."

In reference to the rite in which the Mass was being offered, the Archbishop said that all Catholics, even though they are of different rites, are "one in faith, one in charity, and one in obedience to the Holy See."

He warned against the danger of exaggerated nationalism, the tragic effects of which we have witnessed. "Within the unity of the human race," the Archbishop continued, "there is a variety of characteristics and of cultures among the separate nations. These must be preserved, and the rights of these nations must be respected in justice and charity."

While the year 1945 was in its eventful course, V-J Day dawned and the guns of the world were stilled at last. The day, so long awaited, did not pass without its message from Archbishop Stritch. "Let it be written in human history," he said, "that when attacked we were strong and resourceful in war, but that in our aspirations and in our actions we were Christian peacemakers."

In this year especially, when the time was at hand to announce the annual Peter's Pence collection, the Archbishop's pastoral letter sounded the appeal with vehemence. Perhaps he had seen the Pope's warehouse where gifts were stored that would be disseminated into stricken areas over the face of the earth. "We must help our Holy Father do immense charity," he wrote. "Let us, therefore, in Catholic charity, give until it hurts. God has been very good to us. Our cities, churches, and institutions are intact."

Pius XII as Cardinal Secretary of State had seen our cities, churches, and institutions. The extraordinary journey had brought him forever nearer to our country. His words upon leaving America belonged by anticipation to this year of 1945 and they beat in subtle harmony with the reiterated message of the Archbishop of Chicago.

"May heaven grant," Cardinal Pacelli had said, "that the power of the United States will help to maintain peace in the world. . . . Peace is no more than a temporary truce unless it is transformed into the spiritual bond of the tranquillity of order of which St. Augustine wrote, unless it engages our intellects and hearts in the truth and love of the Pax Dei."

Before the year was over, a message from Pius XII reached not only America, but specifically Chicago. On December 3, 1945, the wires were aflame with news from Rome. Archbishop Stritch was to be elevated to the *Santa Porpora* as one might say in Italy. The ties with Rome were tightening. He was appointed a member of the Sacred College. He would be made a cardinal.

He reacted to this news with characteristic humility. "It pleases me greatly that our Holy Father has so signally honored the Archdiocese of Chicago," the Cardinal-elect announced to his people. "His great kindness shows above everything else his appreciation and esteem for the zeal of my clergy, the faith of my people, and the importance of Chicago. . . ."

XXII

THE Constellation airplane, a giant bird with gleaming silver wings, stood poised ready for flight at the Chicago airport on Sunday morning, February 10, 1946. The Lockheed Constellation of the Transcontinental and World Airlines was about to set out upon its maiden flight from Chicago to Rome, and the Cardinal-designate, whom it was destined to carry, was traveling by air for the first time.

A party of eighteen including four bishops was his escort. They gathered in a little knot about him, with the wind blowing briskly over the open field while his hand was raised in blessing. He sprinkled the plane with holy water. Quietly and distinctly his voice made itself heard through the sudden silence around him: "Let us pray."

"O God, Who hast operated all things for Thy own sake and hast destined all elements of the world for the use of mankind, bless this engine deputed for air journeys in order that it may serve for wider spreading of Thy name's praise and glory and for the prompter expedition of human affairs free from all damages and dangers and fostering heavenly desires in the souls of the faithful using it, through Our Lord. . . . Amen."

Numerous priests and people of Chicago had gathered at the municipal airport to bid their Archbishop good-by. From every corner of the diocese prayers for his safe journey were rising to heaven. Members of the press who were going to Rome in another plane had attended the Mass at the airport, offered by the assistant editor of the *New World*. While the journalists were waiting, the Cardinal-elect spoke to them: "This great dignity which has come to me is a challenge. May the Red Hat of the Cardinal always remind me of the red of the martyr. In serving the Blessed Jesus I shall best serve my country and my city. . . ."

The Cardinal-elect left nothing undone. In a broadcast from the airport, balanced, as it were, on the margin of the world, taking his valiant stand as an international figure, he sent his ringing words flying through the air: "I pray that I am entering a new world-day in which Christian spiritual unity in charity will find its social reflection in a great world unity of genuine democracies."

Detroit was the first stop. Here Archbishop Stritch had a happy reunion with his good friend, the Cardinal-elect, Edward Mooney, who boarded the plane with a group of companions. The two future American Cardinals were on their way to an extraordinary ceremony

The Cardinal's mother

The Cardinal (r) with his brothers, Robert and Eugene

The Cardinal at the age of sixteen
as a minor seminarian

The Cardinal at the time he was
Bishop of Toledo

The Cardinal while in Milwaukee with Bishop William V. O'Connor,
Bishop Roman R. Atkielski, and Bishop Stanislaus V. Bona

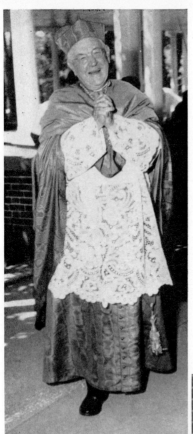

Happy hours were spent
at Maryville

Above, the Cardinal at an Italian summer camp of the Catholic Relief Service sponsored by the N.C.W.C., and, below, his annual visit to the Little Sisters of the Poor

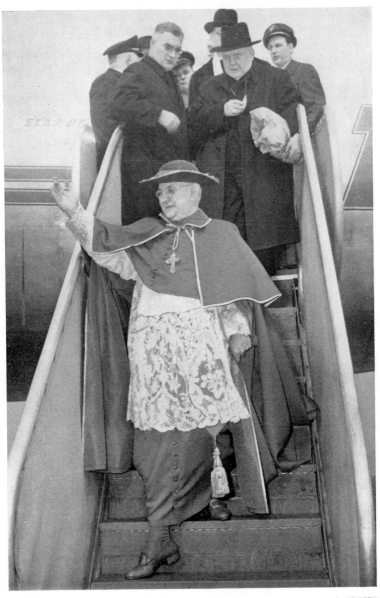

The Cardinal greets the faithful in Chicago upon returning from
Rome after having received the red hat

The Cardinal receives the first blessing of the last class he ordained at St. Mary's of the Lake Seminary at Mundelein

Cardinal Stritch at Mundelein with Cardinal Agaganian

The Cardinal visits the tomb of St. Alphonsus, his patronal saint. Below, he celebrates Mass at St. Agnes Outside the Walls, his titular church

The Cardinal's day begins with Holy Mass in his private chapel

The Cardinal's residence

Breakfast and the morning paper in his study

At the Holy Year Door in St. Peter's with Msgr. Primeau, Archbishop
Cousins, Fr. John Clifford, S.J., dean of faculty at Mundelein, and Bishop
O'Connor of Springfield

The Cardinal at Lourdes

At the dedication of the North American College, His Holiness Pope Pius XII, Cardinals Mooney, Stritch, and Spellman

The Cardinal's last visit to the North American College where he attended school

The family farewell
dinner prior to the
Cardinal's leaving for
Rome

The Cardinal with
his nephew, Fr. Mor-
ris Stritch

The formal reception of the relic of St. Francis Xavier at Holy Name Cathedral

On board the *United States*, Dr. Bergen, Msgr. Hardiman, Archbishop O'Brien, and the Cardinal

The Cardinal on the way to the *Independence* with Cardinal Spellman and Archbishop O'Brien

The Cardinal's last farewell to the U. S.

The Cardinal's last
blessing

The Cardinal's last
thanksgiving

Unless otherwise indi-
cated the pictures are
from the collection of
Rt. Rev. Msgr. James
C. Hardiman to whom
the author and publish-
ers are grateful.

in which more prelates than ever before would be elevated to the College of Cardinals.

"Come back, come back to Rome!" Once more the call of the Pope was alive in the heart of Samuel Stritch. He was coming back. This time another pope dressed in white, but just the same, would place the blood-red hat of the cardinal upon his head. In that Sacred College, closest to the person of the Pope, he was becoming a more intimate part of the Eternal City. Hand in hand, nevertheless, with that deeper intimacy went the power of a fuller dedication to his country beyond the sea. It was for America, not for Rome, that the Pope was making him a cardinal.

XXIII

IN ROME all the lights of St. Peter's were burning on the eighteenth of February, in 1946. Draped in its festive brocades, with its gold and crystals, its marbles and deep-toned mosaics aglow, with a many-colored procession: Swiss Guards and Papal Chamberlains, Noble and Palatine Guards, Prelates, and the Pope on his sedia moving up the stately aisle to the music of silver trumpets, St. Peter's is as near as man's imagination may venture, to the Heavenly City, with a Church triumphant in procession.

Four American archbishops, Cardinals-elect: Glennon, Mooney, Stritch, and Spellman stood together in the presence of the Holy Father while he elevated them, one after another, to the highest dignity that the Church can give. Every cardinal, as is usual, receives a titular church. Cardinal Stritch took the historic Church of St. Agnes-Outside-the-Walls, far up on the Via Nomentana. It was dear to him through more than one association. In it he had offered his first Mass, and Agnes was his mother's middle name. He felt, besides, that St. Agnes was the special patroness of archbishops; for her church is the scene every year of the blessing of the lambs whose wool is made into the sacred pallia, the white circlets that archbishops wear as a symbol of their rank.

The Cardinal's enthusiasm for history and his love for Rome and its monuments lent added attraction to the church. It was built by the Emperor Constantine at the request of his daughter Constantia in honor of the virgin-martyr Agnes who, when little more than a child, was killed during the persecution by Diocletian. It was restored by different celebrated popes, the most recent of whom was Pius IX. It is believed that this is the location once occupied by the patrician home where Agnes lived.

With great joy on February 24, the Cardinal took possession of the church in which as a student he had often prayed and where an ardent Italian welcome awaited him. Printed signs of *Benvenuto al Cardinale Titular* ("Welcome to the Titular Cardinal") adorned the walls of buildings while the surging throng caused a traffic jam. Girl Scouts and Boy Scouts as well as little girls in festive dress lined the Cardinal's approach to the sacristy and with a warm, indulgent smile he gave them his ring to be kissed as he passed. The church was filled with Italians and a number of American prelates and friends, who cheered him as he entered the church and made his way to the throne which had been erected between two precious tapestries.

Archbishop Carinci as Vatican envoy read the papal bull designating this as the titular church of the new Cardinal. Two Americans, Monsignor Kealy, the newly appointed rector of the North American College, and Monsignor Atkielski, chancellor of the Archdiocese of Milwaukee, acted as witnesses to the documents transferring the church to Cardinal Stritch.

After an address of welcome by the pastor of the church, Rev. Mario Marchi, Cardinal Stritch spoke. The story of St. Agnes can do much to "strengthen and inspire Catholics of our times," he maintained. "She has left a glorious example of the lofty ideals of Christianity set for womankind, which does not seem to know that society depends largely for its strength and vitality on the purity of its women. . . . mothers are the real educators of men. . . . we may in all truth say that Agnes has been Christian woman's unfailing inspiration in these days when materialistic humanism . . . is spreading through human society and threatening the very continuance of Christian culture. . . ."

Many visitors called on Cardinal Stritch at the Chicago House, *Santa Maria del Lago* (St. Mary of the Lake) on the Via Sardegna which is not far from a great tourist area and the American Embassy on Via Veneto. This large, comfortable house surrounded by a wall, as most Roman houses are, was a private residence and is the only American diocesan college in Rome. After the foundation of the archdiocesan seminary, St. Mary of the Lake, students for the priesthood from Chicago no longer came to the North American College in Rome for their training. Cardinal Mundelein therefore opened Chicago House for priests of the Chicago Archdiocese who were sent to Rome for postgraduate studies.

One of the great events at Chicago House in its early days was a visit from Cardinal Pacelli, later Pope Pius XII, who in 1935 came to celebrate Thanksgiving Day. The place was closed at the outbreak of World War II, and entrusted to a congregation of religious women. While Cardinal Stritch was in Rome to receive the red hat in 1946, he decided to reopen Chicago House and establish again its prewar scholastic life. Because of a housing shortage in Rome after the war, Chicago House for the first time received priests from other American dioceses.

It is characteristic of the Cardinal that he did not treasure this visit to Rome merely as a profound personal experience. He saw in it another opportunity to interpret the Church to his country and to the world. American that he was, he found in it an occasion to define the position and the responsibilities of his country in face of the world. Loyal as he was, he gave a far-reaching demonstration of the identity of his thinking with that of the Holy Father. From the Vatican radio station on that free territory that rises above all national barriers, in a broadcast to the United States the Cardinal's voice carried his message over land and sea.

"Here in this venerable city of Rome," he said, "a monument witnessing the full story of civilization with its tragedies, triumphs, and the constant challenge of succeeding generations to defend and preserve and rightly interpret Christian truths in terms of changing social conditions, there has been displayed these days the magnificent, inspiring, gripping spectacle of the world unity of the Church.

"Distinguished prelates with their entourages from all parts of the world, of different languages, customs and national affiliations, have met at a solemn ceremony, like sons at home, about our Holy Father Pope Pius XII in the unity of Christ Jesus our Saviour. . . .

"The unity of the Church is not a dull and regimented unity, but a unity in which varieties go to make up one single family in God. In this spiritual Catholic unity there is a variety of offices and a holy equality. . . .

"We believe in the dignity and rights of man and we defend the political equality of all our citizens. . . .

"There can be no compromise with justice; charity must inspire us; hatred and vengeance must be banished from our hearts and minds. Our policy must be to unite all peoples in a world unity of genuine democracy.

"These are the thoughts which are in my mind these days. The spiritual unity of the Church displayed about me opens a vision of a world of free peoples, not dominated and controlled by our country, but inspired by us. . . .

"Relief must not stop with the mere feeding of the hungry and the clothing of the needy; we must reach out with our power and influence to offer to all men the blessings of genuine democracy. The Church will go on with its work; persecutions come, and they only strengthen the spiritual thing in the Church which cannot be touched or injured by might and human tyranny.

"God grant that we, a great people, in these tragic times will make Christian truth shine forth in all our activities and undertakings."

In words such as these the Cardinal writes his own biography. With him, words did not replace action. They directed and identified it.

In early March the Cardinal and his party were ready to return home. At a farewell audience with the Pope on March 4, a correspondent of the Chicago *Herald American*, who accompanied the group, presented His Holiness with an album, bound in white silk, containing a hundred photographs depicting the Cardinal's six years as Archbishop of Chicago.

March storms were not too kind to the airplane beating its way homeward across the Atlantic. When the time for descent preparatory to landing was at hand, the air was opaque. Questioningly the Cardinal looked at the airman who stopped at his seat. "We are looking for a hole in the soup," the officer explained with a wry smile.

In an address to a gathering of nuns, after his return, the Cardinal joked about the bad weather on his trip. "I was glad," he said, "when they found that hole and I could come down to my people and my own home."

That it was good to get back to his people, the next twelve years of intense living would prove beyond question. But it was also good to come down out of a stormy sky to the quiet red-brick mansion. It was good to get back to the warmhearted Sisters, to his books, to Trixie, to the gay little bird in his study.

Unlike his predecessor, the Cardinal did not prefer living in the villa at Mundelein, coming to the city and the chancery to attend to official affairs, then returning to the seminary in its lovely countryside. He remained at Mundelein only when there was work to do, examinations to attend, ordinations to perform, or other business to discharge, and to make his retreat. Then indeed, when all the activity of his being was concentrated within, he was willing to walk among the trees or to sit in solitude beside St. Mary's Lake. The retreat house was, as he said, their powerhouse.

There was another home, however, to which the Cardinal's heart remained faithful and which he visited on March 23. It was his home city of Nashville where he was welcomed for the first time as cardinal with a celebration which lasted two days. In Chicago the enthusiasm for its newly made Cardinal surpassed all bounds in generosity. During the current year the archdiocese raised $1,500,-000 to present to him. The people knew, of course, that the needy would be the real beneficiaries.

And the multiple apostolate continued with vigor, gaining momentum if possible, with each succeeding year. But the wounds of the world were not healing and the Cardinal had to reach out with helping hands, far beyond the confines of his archdiocese though it numbered approximately two million souls. On the other hand, in face of this overwhelming multitude of which he was the shepherd, the Cardinal was always ready to bestow his care upon any individual among them who had a claim upon his help or his sympathy.

This quality was particularly evident when children were concerned. On one occasion, for instance, a little polio victim was sitting contentedly on his knee. On another day he happened to hear from a pastor, who came to the chancery, of a boy of eight in his parish who for two years had been suffering from sleeping sickness. It was not long before the Cardinal took time to visit the stricken home. He climbed three flights of stairs to the attic apartment, fell upon his knees beside the child's bed, and prayed, begging the intercession of St. Jude, the patron of incurable diseases. The boy lay motionless in his deadly sleep, but seemed to smile a little as though something pleasant were happening to him.

XXIV

"HI, CARDINAL!" happy treble voices would ring out when the Cardinal went for a walk on North State Street. "How are you today?" he would ask, smiling down at the children of the neighborhood, circling about him. "O.K.," they would call as they ran off, completely satisfied.

The smile would linger as the Cardinal proceeded down State Street. Often a "panhandler" would see it and shuffle up to him. And the Cardinal, following his usual procedure, would dig into his pocket and empty it of whatever change it carried. Any "bum" could do this to him. In fact, all his private funds went for charity and as cardinal he did not change his habits, in this or in any other way.

He was still the despair of his master of ceremonies. He would step happily out of a procession to pat a child on the head or to speak to some Negro women and children who were standing timidly, a little aside. As someone has said, he believed in observing protocol, except when he wished to break it. A group of Polish women who wanted to talk to him kept him standing for forty-five minutes in front of the Cathedral; and he was quite as interested in speaking to some servicemen in the lobby of a hotel as he was in proceeding to a fashionable meeting upstairs where he was expected.

International affairs also clamored for attention. Tito's hideous regime in Yugoslavia was still aiming at the destruction of the Church. The Cardinal could not remain silent. On the eve of the so-called trial of Archbishop Stepinac of Zagreb, he issued a statement denouncing the indictment of the Croatian Archbishop as a travesty and expressing the hope "that our Government will voice its protest and use its influence in behalf of Archbishop Stepinac and those who with him are victims of this persecution."

Along with Cardinal Griffin, archbishop of Westminster, speaking for the hierarchy of England and Wales, Cardinal Stritch drew attention to the murder of "hundreds of priests, nuns, and helpless citizens" and to the fact that those in control of Yugoslavia seem bent on destroying the Church, "the only remaining voice which can oppose their reign of terror."

It was not difficult for Cardinal Stritch to let his interest shuttle swiftly from one hemisphere to the other. On September 19 he was expressing enthusiastic support of the postwar U.S.O., which he characterized as a spiritual and an intellectual stimulant for those still in service or in hospitals. He joined the President and the Army and Navy chiefs in soliciting aid for the prospective fund-raising campaign in order to continue operations until the end of 1947.

As president of the board of trustees of the National Catholic Community Service which was one of the six member agencies of U.S.O. and at its peak conducted more than 500 U.S.O. operations, the Cardinal took an active part in its administration. He paid personal visits to U.S.O. clubs in many cities, participated in their anniversaries, and blessed their work.

On November 19, 1946, the Apostolic Delegate, Archbishop Cicognani, was in Chicago. Cardinal Spellman came from New York, Cardinal Mooney from Detroit, and Cardinal McGuigan from Toronto to celebrate with Cardinal Stritch the silver anniversary of his episcopal consecration. More than one hundred other prelates and thousands of Catholics thronged the Cathedral for the Pontifical High Mass. In the following passage from his sermon, Bishop Griffin of Springfield, who was the Cardinal's classmate in Rome, brought a reminiscence of the Eternal City to the occasion:

"Educated for the sacred priesthood," he said, "in the very shadow of the cross-crowned obelisks and the lofty cupolas of Catholic

Rome, impressed by the relics of Apostolic times abounding in the catacombs — where martyr-bishops organized the first literal 'underground' against totalitarian oppression — Cardinal Stritch, as have countless Roman students before him and since, learned well the lesson Luther forgot: that it is only in answering loyalty to and uncompromising unity with the Vicar of Christ that men and nations can ever hope to find any meaning at all in the metaphor of the Vine and the branches."

And the Vicar of Christ responded to this unswerving loyalty, in a message signed by him personally, expressing in specific terms for Chicago and the world to hear, his own evaluation of Cardinal Stritch, giving him his place forever in the times in which he lived. The Holy Father said:

"The power of your mind, and the generosity of your heart found full scope and expression in the great see of Chicago, to which you were transferred just when the ominous rumblings of the oncoming war were heard around the world. During the dark years that followed, you showed acute awareness of the pressing difficulties of your own people as well as those of other nations. You strove incessantly to foster religious teachings and social sciences. You widely publicized Papal pronouncements and placed proper emphasis on those treating of harmony among peoples and a just peace.

"Under your expert tutelage, Catholic Action in North America was most fully and effectively developed, especially when as Chairman of the Administrative Board of the National Catholic Welfare Conference you directed monumental works of charity which channeled the relief contributions gathered in the United States to the suffering peoples almost everywhere."

The message concluded by imparting the Apostolic Benediction to the Cardinal, his clergy, and his people.

Before the year 1946 had passed the Cardinal sounded a warning against communist action at home, when he launched his 200,000 Holy Name men into an educational drive against this menace. The Holy Name, this nationwide society of men, was one of the first apostolates to which the Cardinal had directed his attention upon arrival in Chicago, in 1940. To the other objectives of this organization he added a wide program of Catholic Action and constituted the society as the primary Catholic Action agency for the men of the archdiocese. Their program was a dual one: spiritual and cultural. The spiritual side emphasized days of recollection, retreats, all-night vigils on Holy Thursday, the Family Rosary Crusade, the encouragement of the Enthronement of the Sacred Heart in every home, and, most impressive of all, the Holy Hour in the stadium on the lake front when hundreds of thousands came to participate and the Cardinal's usually gentle voice reached them through a loud-speaker.

On the cultural side, one of the principal activities was the lecture bureau which, with help from the universities of the archdiocese, made speakers available for the monthly meetings in parishes. During the war the Cardinal requested the establishment of a military committee in every parish to act as a liaison with the men in the armed forces and, wherever possible, to supplement the work of the chaplains. The membership of the Holy Name Society grew from 66,113 to 253,832 men during the eighteen years of Cardinal Stritch's administration. He himself was frequently at the headquarters signing up new members.

It was this united force that the Cardinal roused into awareness at the annual meeting of the Archdiocesan Holy Name Union, which more than 1000 delegates from approximately 400 parish units attended. In his keynote address he told them that: "Never in the history of the world has there been such an organized effort against God as there is today. I refer directly to communism. . . . The communist followers are like men who are caught in a dream, but do not realize that it is a dream that cannot come true."

XXV

THERE was great commotion in the sunny sky of Texas one early Sunday morning in September, 1947. A squadron of B-25 bombers was circling the margins of Dallas. They fell into formation suddenly when, like a flash of light, a lone plane appeared on the horizon. They flew to meet it and led the way to Love Field in outlying Dallas. A committee of the hierarchy of the Southwest headed by Archbishop Lucey of San Antonio was waiting with Mayor Temple when a slight, gray-haired man with a bright smile stepped from the visiting plane.

The Mayor forthwith presented the keys of the city to Cardinal Stritch while Speaker Reed of the Texan House of Representatives offered the scroll which made the Cardinal a citizen of Texas. Archbishop O'Brien, with a twinkle in his eye, stood at the side. It was not only to become a Texan, however, that the Cardinal had flown to Dallas. He was on his way to preside and preach at a Pontifical Mass at the Cathedral of the Sacred Heart, to dedicate three Catholic schools and an addition to the Guadalupe Mexican Mission.

This was but another demonstration of his availability which did not change when he became cardinal. It was another instance of his willingness to speak and to preach. When his clergy, fearing that he would wear himself out, remonstrated, he replied as before: "It is my ecclesiastical golf. You like to play golf. I like to speak."

Speak he did, often, and on October 27 very forcibly to an audience of women. To concentrate his energies chiefly upon winning men to the service of the Church was far from his intentions. He spent his efforts also upon organizations of women and brought the

85

Archdiocesan Council of Catholic Women to a high point of efficiency in the field of Catholic Action. In stressing the tremendous influence that the Catholic woman exerts within her home and in her neighborhood, he expressed the conviction that we must associate our Catholic Action more with the concrete, everyday things in the community in which we live. In fear of the many destructive influences threatening our American way of life, and in condemning specifically the appeal to the lower instincts in man through amusements and the advertising that goes with them, he called upon the women, especially, to "do a little cleaning up."

Repeatedly he urged Catholics to stand for genuine democracy. "We haven't anything to borrow from strange systems," he said. "We don't need any new principles on which to build our society. We are perfectly content to rest with our own American concept . . . of democracy, but let us make it real. Let us make it actual. Let us assume the responsibilities of citizenship."

New York was having one of its crisp, sunny autumn days, in 1947. A notice in the lobby of the Empire State Building declared the visibility good when the Cardinal from Chicago stepped into the elevator and rode to the eighty-fifth floor. Everyone in the Catholic War Relief office was glad that he had come. Their chief was away in the Near East. Important questions were waiting and there was a general feeling of relief and confidence. The Cardinal would settle them. He had come in fact, to dictate some important letters and promptly seated himself at the desk.

In the adjoining office several undersecretaries were whispering apprehensively to one another:

"I'm afraid to take the dictation." "I hope they won't ask me." "His voice is so soft and pitched so low, I could never catch what he says." "I'll simply have to refuse." In the midst of the chatter the head secretary appeared. "Don't worry," she said cheerily, "I'll take his dictation."

"Can you understand him?" they asked, amazed. "His southern accent and everything?"

The head secretary laughed. "Of course I can; every word. His voice is beautiful and I love his southern accent. Anyhow he's perfectly wonderful."

Never for a moment did the Cardinal raise his voice while he dictated letter upon letter. A lawyer who was in the room listened and noticed that the visitor was using legal terms as fluently as any lawyer could have done.

The Cardinal was dictating letters, some of which required immediate decisions which he was apparently making without hesitation as he went along. His mind was working at white heat; but his voice remained calm and low.

When he was given a memorandum, the functioning was the same. He analyzed it at once and immediately submitted the result. It was a significant day and he spent most of it on the eighty-fifth floor of the Empire State Building, with perhaps an occasional glance at the vibrant city below, at the river that flowed out toward the sea.

Just as untiring as his efforts in war relief, was the Cardinal's work as chairman of the American Bishops' Special Committee to Promote the Pope's Peace Plan. This committee, originally formed in 1941, was reorganized in 1947 to study and publicize the basis for a just peace as laid down by Pope Pius XII. Here the Cardinal's gift for understanding the Holy Father's ideas, for thinking and feeling in accord with him, was of special service during the years following upon the war.

He was keenly aware of the shortcomings of the United Nations since the inception of the charter in San Francisco in 1945, and yet he believed with intense conviction in an international institution of its kind, and that the idea upon which it rests is worth saving, despite the defects in its functioning. Later, however, when Soviet perfidy became apparent and Russia all but wrecked the effectiveness of the United Nations, human resources seemed at an end. Then it was that the Cardinal appealed to his whole archdiocese to pray that the member nations might receive "the light and strength to establish and maintain genuine peace."

Throughout the war, and particularly when the supporters of the Morgenthau Plan were advocating a retribution which would have crushed the life out of Germany, Cardinal Stritch was preaching a peace of justice and charity. A peace of vengeance, a punitive peace was un-Christian and therefore unworkable.

He was consequently in the forefront as a supporter of the Marshal Plan and its manner of aid during the misery and depletion of the postwar years. Like the Holy Father, the condition of the world was of primary concern to Cardinal Stritch; and he applied this concern to all the issues, whether local or universal, that involved persecution or discrimination of any kind. The call that he once issued for "clear thinking and courageous action" reveals the inner quality that is of the essence of his life as a human being and a priest.

XXVI

IN DECEMBER, 1947, the Cardinal left for the deep South. He went first to New Orleans as the special guest of the Jesuits to celebrate the centenary of their return to that city. There were three Jesuits in the Cardinal's family, an uncle and two cousins. The spirit of the Order was therefore akin to him. It even slipped into his letters which invariably bore the heading: A.M.D.G. the *Ad Majorem Dei Gloriam* of Ignatius Loyola.

In New Orleans the Cardinal found two of his great interests combined in Xavier University which is for Negroes and which he regarded as "one of the two or three most important educational undertakings of the Church in the United States." On a visit to this university he addressed some 1100 women students, telling them that the experiences of the past war should convince the United States that one of the great dangers in education is that "we have lagged behind" in the field of science.

"All our advances were in the application of scientific discoveries for the practical need in the way of inventions and mass production," he said. He pointed out that it was European scientists who gave us the principles from which this country developed the atomic bomb and our application of radar. "We have been practical," he admitted, "we have been clever in the invention and production, but we have not been outstanding in the field of pure scientific research."

The same dangers confronting education in science, he added, are also evident in the arts, where "the highest objective is to appreciate and to come to love beauty, for beauty is truth and truth is beauty. We are groping in the artistic field in our own country today, and much of the art talent in our country has been commercialized for producing advertisements. But where there is a seeking for expression of the beauties of our time in art, there is only groping, and that groping, perhaps for the moment, is producing the grotesque."

He had words of enthusiastic praise for Mother Drexel the saintly benefactress of the Negroes, for whom she had founded Xavier University. He complimented also the students for their refusal to listen to the blandishments of "the loudmouthed radicals" in their attempt to "capture the intelligentsia" and to assume leadership of their group by mixing up many truths with many falsehoods.

"They were trying to lead you into paths you have never trod," he told them, "and into paths which were a departure from all that is wonderful and admirable in your nature and temperaments. The only native, artistic culture that we may boast of in the United States is the culture which you have given us in your music and folklore, and that culture is filled with the thoughts and the atmosphere of God. . . . You have brought honor to the Catholic name in the United States, and you have given us a hope and a promise from which there will come great and wonderful things in the future."

It was doubtless his appreciation of the Negro spirituals and his predilection for choral music that led the Cardinal to sponsor a Negro chorus at Xavier, which he later brought to the seminary at Mundelein. His special favorite among the spirituals was: "There is a balm in Gilead, to heal the sin-sick soul."

XXVII

AT THE door of one of the city churches of Chicago early on a chill morning, a man stood waiting. He wore a shabby overcoat that was turning green with age. A dilapidated cap, too small for the massive, shapely head, hung to one side. The shoes were down at the heel and the trousers frayed at the edges.

The janitor's first impulse upon opening the door was to send the man away. Clearly he was a derelict and must have been out all night. But something behind the bloodshot eyes that looked down into his made the janitor think better of it. He said nothing.

The man removed his cap and with an impulsive gesture dipped his hand into the holy-water font, but made no sign of the cross. Without looking at the altar he walked to the farthest corner of the church, sat down in the last pew, and dropped his head upon his hands. Throughout the Mass he did not move. When the priest turned to give the blessing his eye fell upon the strangely huddled figure and, on his way to the sacristy, involuntarily he looked again.

All during breakfast he felt haunted by the man in the last pew. Should he have gone to him? Did the man need help? Returning to the church he approached the man who apparently had not stirred in the interval. He touched his arm. Startled, the man lifted his head and for a moment looked into the eyes of the priest, then turned his head away.

One glance was enough. The priest caught his breath, grasped the man's arm, and held it tight. "Father," he whispered. "Father!" "No longer Father," hoarsely the answer came. "Always Father," the priest replied impulsively. "It is forever." The man trembled. "Tell me," the priest begged. "Tell me everything. Perhaps I can help."

"What there is to tell, you know as well as I." The hoarse voice spoke with effort. "Come with me and we'll have a talk," the priest begged. The man replied: "It's far too late." The look of utter desolation was in his eyes. "Come," said the priest in a tone of command, forcing the man to his feet, and the man came.

"After breakfast," said the priest, "we'll get you into some decent clothes, then you'll feel like yourself."

"Feel like yourself? Which self?" thought the man.

But the priest had not finished. Gradually his erstwhile colleague, the most brilliant of them all, emerged from his psychological coma and the priest took quick advantage. "I think you ought to go to see the Cardinal," he ventured. "The Cardinal!" the other exclaimed in dismay. "His Eminence wouldn't want to see me." "Oh, yes he would. I'm sure of it," the priest insisted.

With lagging steps the prodigal went to the chancery. He had not long to wait. The Cardinal, at sight of him, came forward quickly and put his arms around him. "I have been waiting for you, Father," he said.

XXVIII

"THE only way to get through a banquet," said the Cardinal to his secretary, "is to get through it." The secretary laughed. He had daily evidence of the fact that eating meant very little to the Cardinal. Occasionally he was interested, perhaps in some southern dish or in a plate of ravioli as Italians cook them. In general, however, food did not tempt him. He nibbled rather than ate, a little of this, a little of that, and sometimes at lunch he took nothing but a cup of coffee and a cigarette. It was easy, therefore, to imagine that the long-drawn menu of a banquet was irksome, if not a penance.

There was, however, no escape for the Cardinal. A few instances invite attention, especially since he allowed no such occasion to pass without delivering a message of some kind, either expressing his support of a worthy cause or scoring some destructive influence. On April 6, 1948, he attended a dinner of the Friends of American Relief for Poland, when both he and Mrs. Clare Booth Luce, convert and former congresswoman, received an award for their services toward the relief of Polish war victims. In an address to the 2000 persons gathered in the large dining room of the Stevens Hotel he praised the work of the Polish people, their parishes, and their organizations.

"Poland's heroic fight for Western civilization is known to the world," he said. "Her people have been stanch Catholics through the centuries. They have been fighting for democracy. We must aid them."

At the annual dinner of theater men on September 27 of the same year, he took advantage of the opportunity to administer a rebuke to the movie industry for failing to "meet its social and moral obligations," for catering to "low and debasing appetites in man," and in some measure for the corruption of youth. Far from resenting the criticism, the Theater Owners of America praised the Cardinal's words. At their T.O.A. meeting, following upon the charge that movies frequently give a false impression of life and spread propaganda, the chairman replied that the exhibitors felt encouraged because Cardinal Stritch's remarks coincided with their program to be of greater public service and to encourage the production of motion pictures that would realize more completely the American ideal and the American way of life.

This must have comforted the Cardinal who was by nature averse to giving offense. On the other hand it was equally true of him that when he came to a decision that a thing had to be done, he did it if it killed him. As for the movie industry he had still more to say and he scored as morally disgusting the publicity given to certain star actors whose lives are a pernicious example to all the world. He also cited the annals of juvenile delinquency as demonstrating instances of corruption to youth that came through certain motion pictures. "Your conversion would not be a complete success," he said, "unless you stopped to give serious thought to moral responsibilities in the communities you serve."

In the midst of his pungent criticism, however, the Cardinal had also a word of praise. "I am mindful," he said, "of the good films and the contributions these have made to the public welfare."

He raised his voice in warning again, though on a totally different matter, on October 16, 1948, at the convention in Chicago of the National Alliance of Czech Catholics. This alliance had co-operated with the War Relief Services of the National Catholic Welfare Conference in securing guarantees of jobs and homes for displaced persons of Czech or Slovak descent and had been undertaking the care of thousands of refugees who escaped from Czechoslovakia since the communist coup in February of 1948.

Propagandists were trying to produce the impression that the Red regime in Czechoslovakia is friendly toward religion and wishes to see freedom throughout the world. In answer to this the Cardinal had the following to say: "These propagandists are very clever in the use of words and in the presentation of certain facts and suppression of other facts. It is particularly important that you keep yourself informed, and that you be not led astray by half-truths, which will be circulated and are being circulated." The Cardinal urged furthermore that the Alliance support the Nepomucenum, the Czech college in Rome for the training of priests. "As long as the Nepomucenum exists," he said, "there will be priests in Czechoslovakia."

The delegates pledged that the Alliance would extend all possible help to displaced persons and be brother to them in their need, particularly to those with whom they are associated by bonds of religion, culture, and ancestry. In further resolutions they stressed Christian principles as the foundation of general good will among the peoples of all creeds and cultural backgrounds. The resolutions concluded: "We shall co-operate with all citizens of good will under the direction of our spiritual and civic leaders, i.e., National Catholic Welfare Conference and National Alliance of Czech Catholics."

The Cardinal must have gone home satisfied.

XXIX

IT WAS late afternoon in Rome. Siesta time lasted a little longer during the summer months when the sun was strong. It was the hour of promenade and a slight breeze from the Apennines was scattering whiffs of refreshment into the heat of the day. The fortresslike doors that guarded the entrance to Chicago House on the Via Sardegna swung open and Cardinal Stritch with one of his young priests came out for his afternoon walk. Numerous occasions in addition to his *ad limina* visits brought the Cardinal to Rome. Besides, it was the alternate home of his spirit and he loved it at all seasons as the following excerpt from a letter testifies:

"I know that summer is not a good season at Rome; but I am used to Rome at all times and love it as much 'nei calori di San Lorenzo' as 'nella primavera di Sant' Agnese.'" (He loved it as much in the heats of St. Lawrence as in the spring of St. Agnes.)

"Let's go up to the Aventine," he suggested to his companion. "The view is so fine from there." Just as he had done many a time on all the seven hills of Rome, the Cardinal retraced the walks of his student days along the quiet, residential streets of the Aventine: to the old church of St. Alexis; to pillared Santa Sabina where St. Dominic's body rests and the friars were chanting office; to Sant'-Anselmo of the Benedictines, also filled with the singing voices of monks, with the Abbot Primate at their liturgical Hours.

Last of all they stopped at the iron gates of the mother house of the Knights of Malta and peered through the giant keyhole with its glorious surprise: St. Peter's in a direct line, on the lower Vatican

Hill. "These gates look as though they never open" the young priest said. A spirit of mischief crept into the Cardinal's eye. "Do you want to see what a cardinal's band can do for you?" he asked. At that he rang the bell and when the old porter saw the red girdle of a cardinal at the keyhole, the gates opened as though by magic and an enchanting garden disclosed itself, lying in a fullness of sunlight.

As usual, however, when the Cardinal was in Rome, he did not spend all his time taking walks or demonstrating what a cardinal could do. On the twelfth of August he was at a press conference where he had various things to say. "I am very proud of what my country has done in Italy and elsewhere in the world for the relief of human suffering and the reconstruction of a free Christian world," he told the reporters. He also answered their questions on his observation of conditions in Italy. "Prescinding from the large economic problems," he said, "I find the people generally looking better, healthier and more active than in 1946. They are working, doing things. Reconstruction has gone very far."

In reference to American aid and its influence, he said: "As long as we remain strong, firm champions of our own democracy, we will be doing the best thing for the world. There should be no compromise with totalitarianism, for there can be no good world without recognition of human rights. . . ."

He alluded to the contribution of American Catholics to the work of relief and estimated that the separate contribution made by Catholics of the United States in the preceding year amounted to about seven million dollars. He told the reporters that he considered the condition of the Church in the United States as flourishing. He said also that the Catholics of our country showed no real surprise at the decree of the Holy See against communism: "They accepted it as an act of the Holy Father which was very well advised and showed once more the Church's position regarding atheistic communism."

He told them that the immigration program for displaced persons was successful so far as the Archdiocese of Chicago is concerned; that the See of Chicago had found homes and jobs for about

1700 displaced persons so far, and since additional ones were arriving every week, expected to provide for many more. The Chicago Archdiocese had also helped about 3000 displaced persons on their way through the city to other destinations.

The high point of the Cardinal's visit to Rome came on the day of the twenty-eighth anniversary of his nomination as bishop, when the Pope received him with a warm welcome. He had occasion to tell His Holiness of the sacrifices that Americans were making in helping Europeans; that they were giving a much larger amount of their ordinary means to this relief than the average European realizes. He pointed out that Americans contributed to this relief both through tax money and through voluntary gifts.

It was during this visit to Rome that the Cardinal conceived the idea of giving something useful to St. Peter's. A consultation with Monsignor Kaas, superintendent of the basilica, revealed the fact that he and his assistants had been investigating the possibility of using some type of scrubbing machine to solve the difficult problem of cleaning the church. According to the time-honored method of marble dust, cleanser, sawdust, water, brooms, and elbow grease, six men had to spend three months to complete the thorough cleaning of the 24,000 square yards of marble floor. The Cardinal came to the rescue by promising to send two good scrubbing machines from Chicago.

The machines were sent. Monsignor Kaas was completely satisfied and, thanks to the Cardinal, the Sanpietrini or maintenance men of St. Peter's were happy. The machine, operated by one man and a helper, could do the work in one week.

In the meantime the Cardinal's charities at home did not abate. With every Christmas, for one thing, 100 poor boys ranging from 4 to 14 continued to receive the gift of a complete outfit of clothing. This event was always accompanied by a Christmas party. The clothing alone was valued at $10,000.

XXX

FOR some time the Cardinal had been sitting at his desk with his finger up against his nose, a sure sign that he had a problem. Cigarette after cigarette was lit and left unfinished — another indication of profound preoccupation. The Stritch School of Medicine of Loyola University was in difficulties.

The Cardinal had come to the rescue of the Loyola Medical School on a former occasion when there was danger of its being forced to discontinue and it had since assumed his name. Realizing the great need of a well-equipped Catholic medical school, he had appealed to the parishes, taken a hand in its financing — in short he had made it his own project. Since so expensive an undertaking usually operates at a loss, there was need for further planning.

Under pressure of this necessity the Cardinal evolved a unique expedient: he sent an attractive invitation to a goodly number of the citizens of Chicago with the following explanation and message:

"His Eminence, the Archbishop of Chicago, is faced at times with urgent extraordinary needs of the Archdiocese. To meet these needs his only material resource is the charity of his people and friends.

"In inviting a group of his people and friends to have dinner with him he is asking each one who attends to make a donation in the amount of $250.00 to help him meet a present urgent need not only of religion in the Archdiocese but also of our community. This need is to discharge the deficit in the operating expenses of the Stritch Medical School. He hopes that the contribution given by his guests at this dinner will be sufficient for this purpose. . . .

"His Eminence gives the assurance on the guarantee of the Blessed Master that the spiritual returns for this charity will be a hundredfold."

As the year 1949 was nearing its end the Cardinal was with the Back-of-the-Yards Neighborhood Council once more, and again he had to attend a dinner; but it gave him an opportunity to tell the people of this great "melting pot" that a return to the old neighborly spirit would do more to destroy the Marxist political philosophy than anything else. He cited as examples the old custom of visiting neighbors, caring for the sick, lending a cup of sugar or a loaf of bread as potent weapons in the fight to preserve and extend democracy.

This "Packingtown" of Chicago, which the council represents, is a veritable international settlement of 100,000 persons including Czechs, Germans, Irish, Lithuanians, Poles, and Slovaks.

The year closed with a citation for the Cardinal: the Leo XIII Award of the Scheil School of Social Studies for "outstanding devotion to the cause of Christian Social Education." The citation said in part: "To the spirit of the early missionary, Cardinal Stritch has added the modern apostle's perception of the special role of the Church in our time. He has demanded for all men everywhere, the reality of justice and the reality of charity."

This attention that Cardinal Stritch gave to social problems was not confined to conditions among Catholics of the archdiocese; rather it was of benefit to the entire city of Chicago. The Interracial Council and the Cardinal's Conservation Committee which was established expressly for the purpose of preventing the growth of slums, were two permanent forces that contributed to the betterment of living conditions in Chicago. Furthermore, as the Catholic Charities expanded and gave certain services that could not be obtained from secular agencies, the Cardinal made them available also to non-Catholic citizens. One of the secular papers of Chicago has called attention to the Cardinal's service to the city during a time of great change. Changing neighborhoods brought problems in housing while many newcomers to the city created problems in human relations.

This expansive attitude on the part of the Cardinal no doubt communicated itself to the laity of the archdiocese. In an article entitled: "CHICAGO — The Country's Biggest Diocese Fathers a New Approach to Contemporary Problems," the September, 1956, issue of *Jubilee Magazine* quotes the Cardinal as saying that a bishop "must associate with himself good, generous lay souls, for he must understand that his work is so large that he cannot do it himself. . . . What a blessing it is for a Bishop to have a group like this to help him in his work. . . . I have always had a realization that I need you." In keeping with this spirit, the above-mentioned article observes that a distinguishing characteristic of the lay apostolate in Chicago is its outward look. Besides the personal sanctification of their members, the various groups aim at city-wide reform of social institutions. "Chicagoans," the writer of the article continues, "are proud of the 'total view' which has marked their apostolate."

It is this "total view" which was so characteristic of the Cardinal himself. At the Red Mass of the Catholic lawyers, for instance, he would speak to them in their own legal terms. Interested as he was in all the developments in medicine, when he addressed the American Medical Association he used the language of their profession, and all of this with perfect ease. When he met with financiers and businessmen they marveled at his familiarity with the world of finance and at his business acumen.

He was chancellor not only of a missionary society, the Extension, but also of the two universities, Loyola and De Paul, and the teaching Christian Brothers made him their affiliate. His orbit included examinations for the doctorate at the seminary in Mundelein when he addressed the candidates in flawless Latin and it included also doing something constructive for the outcasts of Skid Row. His total view and the diversity of action that resulted from it is a challenge to the imagination. And yet, in his presence all grew calm and the sound of his quiet voice banished all sense of speed or breathlessness.

XXXI

THE dazzling sun of California had looked down upon many a gallant cavalcade, on many a picturesque forty-niner, while old Sutter's Mill in Sacramento circled merrily, and Market Street in San Francisco was built wide to accommodate the parades of the gold-rush days. But never before had it shone upon the red robes of a cardinal on an official visit, until Cardinal Stritch came in September of 1950 to celebrate the centenary of the first parish in California, established in Sacramento.

He presided at the Mass offered by Bishop Armstrong of Sacramento outdoors in the county-fair grounds. Once more there was a procession, with the Cardinal in his long red train as its climax. Throngs waited to see him pass. He was still for protocol except when he wanted to break it, and that was precisely what he wanted to do on this festive outdoor day.

While scattering smiles and blessings among the people, he spotted a familiar face from Chicago in a group of booksellers. "Hello, Gene," he said as he passed. "How is the book business?" Then his eye fell upon some colored children clustered about their mother. Leaving the ranks he went over to bless them. At this the crowd swarmed around him until those in charge of affairs became alarmed. "No," he said with his gentle voice, "don't worry about it. They simply want to see a cardinal."

In Chicago on a later day there also was a procession; but one that delayed long before getting started. The Cardinal did not break protocol but stood and waited with folded hands. Finally, turning to the monsignor beside him with a humorous air of patience, he said: "It seems to me I spend half of my life waiting."

The year 1950 had come. A year of jubilee, a Holy Year! On the day of Christmas Eve the Pope had struck with his golden mallet and the Holy Door of St. Peter's was opened. Already the multitudes on their knees were passing over its sacred threshold. The Holy Doors of the three other great basilicas likewise stood open and the year of grace, of penance, and propitiation had begun.

Longing was in the heart of the Cardinal. "Come back, come back to Rome," the call of the Pontiff was sounding within him again. He did go back. This was a different return. Rome, eternally the same yet always having something new to give! He had preached, he had labored that peace and healing might come to the stricken world. Now it was time to pray, perhaps as never before. The gates of heaven were opening and the ear of God came close.

With some of his bishop-friends near him he knelt as a pilgrim on the threshold of the Holy Door from which one sees St. Peter's as with newly awakened eyes. Ceaselessly the faithful came and went, priests with their people from far and near, processions moving slowly behind their cross-bearers, praying, singing — a Pentecost of different tongues speaking words that were the same.

The Holy Year had run only halfway through its course when a sorrow came to the Cardinal. In July, 1950, Sister Fredericka died. For twenty years she had been "the Angel in the House" to him, the mother heart that made it home, a familiar presence that never obtruded itself, but was always at hand, quiet, efficient, warm. The Cardinal had the type of sensitivity that never wanted to ask you to do anything; but was delighted when you wanted to do it. He never needed to ask Sister Fredericka and she always gave without the asking. Her religious dedication had expressed itself in the perfection of her service to him and to his household. As deeply as he appreciated her, so deeply did he miss her and mourn her loss.

In America again, the highly charged life continued. There was scarcely a week, for instance, that the Cardinal did not address some group of educators. During his years in Chicago he not only established many new parishes, but he built numerous schools. Continuously he preached that Catholic schools are not an end in themselves, but only a means to help their students correspond with God's grace in learning how to live thoroughly Catholic lives. To have every Catholic child in a Catholic school was his ideal and with this he meant all Catholic children, rich and poor, intelligent and dull, Negro and white, well behaved and mischievous. He urged also that Catholic schools take care of their problem children and not turn them over to public schools. Repeatedly he said that the Church never runs away from problems; but stays with them until they are solved.

Believing that the home exercises a stronger influence than the school he recommended that teachers keep in close communication with parents and that there be an organization of home and school associations in all parish schools. "Covet parents' constructive criticism," he told teachers and suggested that adjustments in school practices be made to accord with reasonable wishes on the part of parents.

Ever since 1941 Cardinal Stritch had made his own the great dream of St. Pius X concerning catechetical instruction. Shortly after coming to Chicago he organized the Confraternity of Christian Doctrine and appointed a director with instructions to set up a diocesan catechetical office for the development of better and more efficient catechetical methods. During the following year 2221 public school children were enrolled in a program of religious instruction known as the Released-Time Program. By the year 1957, 47,533 children of elementary public schools were receiving religious instruction.

In the meantime many years, under the Cardinal's guidance, went into study and experimentation for the instruction of pupils on the secondary-school level. From the social-instructional program beginning in 1943, the work developed into a systematic four-year program of religious guidance known as the Parish High School of

Religion. There were those who feared that this efficient system of religious instruction would make parents feel justified in sending their children to public schools. The Cardinal disagreed and he proved to be right; for many students, owing to this catechetical instruction, eventually enrolled in Catholic schools.

In 1948 he had supported the plan of several priests, which was to advertise Catholic Information Classes in the daily newspapers and in vehicles of transportation. With the resulting increase in parish Information Classes the Cardinal placed them as a charge of the Confraternity of Christian Doctrine. In 1952, furthermore, the Paulist Fathers requested permission to advertise their Home Study Course. At the Cardinal's suggestion they united their advertising with that of the Information Classes, and later, in 1955, he placed this school for non-Catholics also under the direction of the Confraternity of Christian Doctrine. In 1957, 6790 Chicagoans were requesting these Home Study Courses by mail, and in 1958 the number mounted to 10,000.

This result justified the Cardinal's belief that the Church should place the resources of modern techniques at the service of the Faith. It is further evidence of the underlying fact in the Cardinal's life, that he was first and essentially the priest and that to him all other talents were of no account except insofar as they ministered to the priestly talent that God had given him.

It is thrilling to feel an awareness of a subtle relationship between two scenes, one in Rome years ago, and one in Chicago in 1951. In Rome on Sunday mornings in the court of St. Damasus, St. Pius X, surrounded by children of the city, instructed them in catechism. In Chicago, almost a half century later, an enormous throng of delegates from all over the country crowded the Stadium for the National Conference of the Confraternity of Christian Doctrine. In the silence of rapt attention they caught fire for further apostolic effort from the flame-tipped words of Bishop Fulton Sheen and from the quiet light that burned in the voice of the Cardinal. Truly the mustard seed had grown into a tree.

XXXII

A HAPPY smile wreathed the Cardinal's face when he looked up from a letter bearing the postmark of Vatican City and signed by Cardinal Fumasoni-Biondi, Prefect of the Sacred Congregation for the Propagation of the Faith. There was no shadow of prophecy in his joy after reading the contents which promised the solution of a long-standing problem.

The Roman Cardinal was presenting the Catholic Auxiliaries, a unique lay missionary society, to Cardinal Stritch, and explaining their work, which is to train young women and send them to missionary countries that they may assist the people and thereby cooperate in spreading the Kingdom of God among pagans.

The presence in Chicago of many Catholic students from the missionary countries of the world had caused him serious worry because there was no Catholic group in the city, devoted exclusively to their care. As a result these students often drifted away from the Church and returned to their homes as fallen-away or lukewarm Catholics.

Cardinal Stritch responded warmly to this appeal and in 1951 welcomed the society into the diocese. Thereupon the Auxiliaries opened Crossroads Student Center near the University of Chicago, for the purpose of providing spiritual and material aid to Catholic and non-Catholic foreign students and to supply for them a "home away from home." In 1953 upon the encouragement of the Cardinal they established a center for training young women who wished to become members of their society. For three years this center was located in a large home at 1103 N. Dearborn Street, which belonged to Catholic Charities.

Some years later when referring to his concern for the foreign students, the Cardinal said: "To take care of these people was a pressing obligation. And when these Lay Auxiliaries came along, it seemed like the answer to a problem, and at once we did what we could to set them up."

They did not disappoint him. His appreciation as well as his own world-wide missionary concern is evident in the following words: "I think the biggest thing these missionaries have done for us in Chicago has been to stick a pin to us to make us realize our Catholicity, to help us widen the reaches of our charity, to make us understand that we have a personal interest, every one of us, in the success of the work of the Redemption — in Vietnam, in China, and even in those countries over which there is darkness . . . today."

The year 1951 also brought to fruition a practical dream of a certain monsignor who came to the Cardinal one day with a plan. It was a proposal to build a special retreat house with all facilities under one roof, on the seminary grounds at Mundelein, so that instead of the two crowded annual retreats during the summer, the priests might have retreats throughout the year. "Go and try," said the Cardinal, ready as always to give anyone a free hand in carrying out a creative idea.

The monsignor did, with the result that in 1951 he directed the building, on 90 acres of the seminary grounds, of a retreat house that could accommodate approximately 50 priests and that has since been enlarged. Every week a new group comes and outstanding preachers from England and Ireland as well as from America are provided as retreat masters. The Cardinal gave special attention to the design, the decoration, and the furnishings of the chapel. His feelings are reflected in a letter of gratitude to a specially generous monsignor and pastor:

"I thank you very much for your letter and for your expression of appreciation of our Clergy Retreat House. Nothing these days has given me greater consolation than the many letters which have come to me from priests who made retreats at our Retreat House for the Clergy.

"I thank you very, very much for your gift of two thousand dollars for the glass window which will be of St. Gregory the Great in our Retreat House Chapel. It is a beautiful thing that this offering is in thanksgiving for the many blessings bestowed on St. Gregory's Parish and its priests.

"I thank you very much also for your generous offering of one thousand dollars for one of the Stations of the Cross in our chapel and I want to say that this offering is all the more appreciated because you make it as an offering for wayward priests. When I have the opportunity I shall stress this intention at our Retreat House."

In an article in the *Osservatore Romano*, the semiofficial newspaper of the Vatican, Cardinal Piazza of the Sacred Consistorial Congregation, a department charged with the supervision of dioceses, gives enthusiastic praise to the Retreat House and the forward thinking of the Church in America to which it gives expression.

From an article in the *Osservatore Romano* to an article written exclusively for the International News Service is a far cry. To swing from Cardinal Piazza to Louis Bromfield requires wide range. We have the famous novelist, Louis Bromfield to thank when, under the arresting title: "Personalities Dominate Convention," he gives us his impression of the Cardinal as he appeared at the national political convention held in Chicago on July 9, 1952.

"One of the fascinating things about a national political convention," writes Mr. Bromfield, "is the personalities of the candidates and the big shots and their effect upon the delegates and the public.

"You can feel it even when the personality or candidate in question has not even made an appearance in the huge auditorium at the stockyards." After commenting upon General MacArthur, Senator and Mrs. Taft, General Eisenhower and his wife, Mr. Bromfield continues:

"But of all the personalities which have up to date appeared before the convention, the most moving and impressive was a small white-haired old gentleman with a kind of radiant beauty in his face and an air of dignity and grace which was overwhelming.

"He was Cardinal Stritch, Archbishop of Chicago, who delivered the invocation at the third session of the convention.

"The invocation itself was one of the most beautiful pieces of writing I have ever been privileged to hear, filled with beauty, dignity, honor and simplicity. The Cardinal is a small man but when he walked onto the platform in the huge convention hall every one of the thousands of spectators was aware that the man who moved toward them was somebody.

"Under quite different circumstances, his entrance was perhaps more impressive than that of General MacArthur. There was no escort, no flags, no trumpet calls but it is quite possible that the Cardinal brought with him something greater and more impressive . . . the presence of God, which we need so badly in this country at this time in the history of the world."

"A great percentage," Mr. Bromfield concludes, "of the politicians now present in Chicago, now working underground, now making speeches, might well profit by studying the personalities of these four men, to discover that of all the forces in politics and in the world, the greatest are honor and simplicity.

"It is what makes the difference between the great and the shabby and mediocre."

XXXIII

"WHERE is the Cardinal? Hasn't he gotten here yet?" the architect of St. Patrick's High School asked, approaching a knot of workmen. "There he is, way up there," one of them answered pointing to a ladder propped against a wall of the unfinished building. He had climbed up a carpenter's ladder and was making a leisurely survey of what had been done since his last visit. When the Cardinal heard the architect's voice the ladder began to vibrate as he swung down almost with the same agility that characterized him as a walker.

St. Patrick's was a pet of his. From its inception to its completion, when important persons came to the city he took them to see it. It was the first high school of modern design in the new high school building program, and he had a personal feeling toward it. With him architecture was a hobby.

Catholic Charities in the meantime was penetrating into problems other than those of poverty until its beneficence came into contact even with the educational system; for the Cardinal created a whole new field of specialized services. Perhaps the secret of its success was the spirit of love, so plainly evident as the source of the efficient performance, that made things grow in every shadowed corner of the archdiocese. Experts sent by the Charities came into parochial schools to test regularly the sight and hearing of every child so that defects might be remedied before it was too late. In existing parish schools the Cardinal established four day schools for deaf and three for blind children, so that by means of the latest technical equipment and teaching by Sisters who are specialists, the handicapped children, happily adjusted, may take their places in regular classes.

The Catholic Charities Guidance Center where children receive medical, psychological, or psychiatric care, the Cardinal's committee for the Spanish-speaking, the Catholic Guild for the Blind, Loyola Center for Child Guidance, the Peter Maurin House for the rehabilitation of alcoholics, all are part of this far-reaching program of charity. "So far as the Catholic Charities are concerned," a staff member observed, "His Eminence may be in Rome — but his presence will be felt everywhere in his charitable accomplishments. Thus deeply has Samuel Cardinal Stritch left upon his charities the imprint of his own love for the unfortunate."

Perhaps tact is also a part of charity. At any rate there is tact in a letter of October 20, 1952, which the Cardinal wrote to the pastors of the archdiocese:

"In asking for voluntary offering of the faithful of a parish for the support of the Parish Church and its works, very great care must be used to avoid anything which has the semblance of an obligatory admission fee. Several times the Holy See has forbidden the requiring at church doors of a fee for attending Holy Mass. The so-called Church seat collections must be wholly voluntary and the faithful must be informed that there is no monetary requirement for attending Holy Mass. Those who for one reason or another cannot make an offering and even those who do not wish to make an offering enjoy full freedom to assist at Holy Mass in our Churches."

In 1953, with the conviction that sacred music was necessary to the dignity of Church services, the Cardinal set up a Commission on Sacred Music in the Archdiocese of Chicago.

He made repeated efforts to promote education in music throughout the schools of the archdiocese. "We must have more music and better music in our schools," he asserted, "for education without music is poor education indeed." The Commission, which began its functioning in 1953, immediately entered upon a careful study of the matter and under the authority of the Cardinal issued directives planned to assist in the development of music that would contribute to the beauty and decorum of Church services.

The Cardinal took further steps in authorizing the establishment of an archdiocesan unit of the National Catholic Music Educators Association. The unit was named the Chicago Catholic School Music Association and given the objective of carrying out in education the plans of the Archdiocesan Commission on Sacred Music. Recognition from educators in music throughout the country came later when the National Catholic Music Educators Association invited Cardinal Stritch to become its honorary president.

The Commission on Sacred Music took its obligations seriously. It had been working, as the Cardinal said publicly, "to enhance the beauty of the sacred liturgy and bring a uniformity to our music." Upon its recommendation the Cardinal eventually placed a ban upon playing the wedding marches of Wagner and of Mendelssohn in the churches of the archdiocese. Eight versions of the *Ave Maria*, including the famous Bach-Gounod arrangement, were also forbidden as well as songs like "I Love You Truly," "O Promise Me," and "Because." In a letter appearing in the *New World*, the Cardinal said: "No deviation can or will be permitted."

The Cardinal's various letters alone would make a long, long story, while his pastorals are a world in themselves. Despite the public appearances on his schedule, of which there were between four and five hundred a year, in addition to the office hours at the chancery and the complex affairs of the diocese, the writing of letters played an important part in the Cardinal's daily routine.

They were his first duty in the morning upon arrival on the second floor of the chancery where his mail and his lay secretary awaited him. Slowly and precisely he dictated the letters that could be discharged at once, keeping much of the correspondence, perhaps 25 to 50 letters, for the evening at home in his study. He ordinarily used a dictating machine for his faithful home secretary, Sister Mary Alacoque. The remainder he typed himself, composing as he typed. Every serious letter received a personal reply and with two speedy fingers he usually acknowledged even unimportant letters, even birthday cards and post cards.

His pastorals came directly from his own heart, not from that of another. The one on prodigals for instance, written in 1955, pulsates with the agony of a Shepherd for the wayward sheep and carries a strong echo of the Master's voice saying: "Them also must I bring." Profoundly the Cardinal felt that he was responsible even for the sheep that had strayed and that he must bring them back to the flock. So acute was his concern that he begged for special public prayers in the churches of the archdiocese in reparation and for the return of the prodigals.

This appeal and the pastoral on the Blessed Sacrament were perhaps the most moving of the Cardinal's letters to the parishes. When the latter was read from the pulpit it happened that a visiting Claretian Father was saying the Mass. He was so deeply impressed that he went home with an unshakable conviction. "The man who wrote that," he told his fellow Claretians, "is a saint."

XXXIV

CARDINAL STRITCH and Bishop O'Connor, rector of the North American College in Rome, were standing in front of the entrance to the new North American College on the Janiculum on Wednesday, October 14, 1953, awaiting the approach of a shining black car, that betokened an event unprecedented in the history of Rome since Pius IX had left the Quirinal to imprison himself in the Vatican. Those who saw the black car in its passing knelt in the street or on the curb while a hand, slender, beautiful, and vital, was raised in benediction and a face that the people loved smiled in greeting. Cries of "*Il Papa, il Papa*" still echoed from the street while the car swung up the slope of the Janiculum.

The Cardinal and the Bishop fell upon their knees, kissing the Fisherman's ring as Pius XII alighted. The ecclesiastical embrace followed and the Pope with quick step walked up the short stair to the entrance where he stood for a moment looking out over Rome. It was long since he had seen his city from the top of the Janiculum, spread out before him in a panorama that no other city in the world has to offer.

Ever since the concordat between Pius XI and Mussolini for which Cardinal Merry del Val had so skillfully prepared the way, the Pope was no longer a prisoner. Pius XII nevertheless made but little use of his freedom except on extraordinary occasions as when he went unafraid into the midst of the chaos that the war had brought upon Rome and bent over the dying and the dead. Or again when he visited the Church of the Jesuits which, during the war, sheltered the image of the *Madonna del Divino Amore* (Madonna of the Divine Love). It was she, the Italians felt, who had saved the Eternal City and the Holy Father went in person to thank her.

That the Pope should come to the new North American College on the day of its dedication was a gracious gesture toward America, and all the gratitude and all the love of America radiated in the eyes of Cardinal Stritch as he knelt at the feet of His Holiness. His attitude, more than words could have done, expressed his profound humility, his spirit of loyalty and affectionate reverence. The Pope, with the Cardinal's hands clasped in his, leaned forward in his chair and spoke like a father does to his son. The photograph taken of the scene was so moving, and conveyed so completely the accord that existed between these two greathearted human beings that an Italian artist made a painting from it, capturing forever the spirit of this relationship. The painting was sent to America and hung in the dining room of the Cardinal's home in Chicago just opposite his place at table.

Cardinal Stritch was on his *ad limina* visit. Happily the occasion coincided with the dedication of the new campus of his Roman Alma Mater. The house on Via Umiltà, so dear to the memory of many an American priest and bishop, is still retained for American priests doing postgraduate work.

Cardinal Stritch delivered the address at the dedication ceremonies, reminding Americans of the ideals upon which their country was established, referring everything basically to the recognition of the dignity which God has given to man.

His opening words must have struck a sympathetic note in the hearts of all Americans present. "Some few years after the end of the First World War" he began, "returning home from Europe, I stood with three American priests at the rail of the ship as we came into New York Harbor. The day was dark and dank. A heavy mist hung over everything. Finally the Statue of Liberty came into view. One of my companions turned to me and said: 'Bishop! She may have her faults, but she is the best there is.'"

"When we speak of our country," the Cardinal continued, "what is it that we have in our minds and heart? Is it our fertile plains beside our river courses? Is it our mountains with their mineral treasures? Is it our vast stretches of ranch lands with their subsoil riches? Is it even that standard of living which no other people have ever achieved? For all these things we humbly thank God and beg of Him the grace to use them aright. But they are not the things we have in mind when we think of our country. For us our country above everything else is a land of freemen, conscious of their rights and dignity, collaborating together in a brotherly spirit for the common good of all."

Patriotism expanding into peace; peace everywhere, based upon justice and charity which in turn rest upon the Divine Law; these are the concepts springing forth under the impact of the Cardinal's words.

XXXV

THE speakers' table in the great banquet hall of the Conrad Hilton Hotel stood in a glory of candlelight, chrysanthemums, and red decorations on the evening of November 14, 1953. Above the table hung the Cardinal's coat of arms with the Latin escutcheon: *Deus Meus Adjutor Meus* (My God Is My Helper). A magnificent procession of Church dignitaries and knights preceded the dinner which was becoming an annual highlight in the social and civic life of Chicago. This year, as usual, one thousand persons contributed $250,000 to the Cardinal's charities among which the Stritch School of Medicine and the Lewis Memorial Maternity Hospital were the principal beneficiaries. A generous private person paid all the expenses of the banquet, so that not a penny of the money given by the guests was diverted from the charities for which the Cardinal intended it.

Eventually his keen eye singled out an unexpected group for apostolic attention and made his annual dinner serve an added purpose. Hitherto nothing had been done socially for the Catholic debutantes of Chicago in an outspokenly Catholic way. Many of them as a result found their places in the non-Catholic social world. In the brilliant annual dinner the Cardinal found the remedy.

In earlier years the debutantes accompanied the knights in the festive procession. Later the Cardinal made the dinner the occasion of introducing them into society under Catholic auspices, thereby turning their lives into a different direction. This little stroke of apostolic diplomacy tallies well with the Cardinal's manner of handling visitors, according to Mr. Dan Herr writing in the *Sign* magazine where he quotes an associate "who has hobnobbed with career diplomats from all over the world" as maintaining that most statesmen "look like amateurs compared to His Eminence" and that "he's a Roman diplomat with a touch of black-eyed peas and hominy-grits."

The Cardinal himself revealed his attitude toward social functions when, after an impressive religious ceremony, he said: "This is what I love. Tonight I must attend a banquet. It is my hair shirt; but I must do it to help my poor." Nevertheless no outward evidence of the hair shirt was perceptible in the genial host who received one thousand people on this November evening.

"I shall keep you in my prayers and in my love," he told his guests, "and our Saviour will keep you in His love. I guarantee that you have never made a better investment than tonight."

He stressed education and medical care for all, as one of the community's greatest needs. "If we are going to have the doctors our community needs," he said, "we must foot some of the bills to provide them the education. You here are contributing to the welfare of the thousands of persons whom the doctors will serve. To get the finest doctors we must provide for the finest schools."

He also gave his guests news of the Holy Father whom he had seen in the preceding month: "I saw the Pope and talked with him, noting his strong voice and his magic smile. I saw in his calm face the truth of Almighty God, a force that can withstand the onslaughts of atheistic communism, a force that dictators cannot destroy."

Every one of the guests, Catholic and non-Catholic, received a rosary blessed by the Pope, and in addition a photograph of the Pope and Cardinal Stritch taken at the time of their audience.

Both Governor Stratton of Illinois and Mayor Kennelly had pertinent things to say of the Cardinal, things indicating his stature not only as a churchman but also as a civic leader.

His leadership came to the surface again at a meeting of the Catholic Lawyers' Guild of Chicago, when he scored severely the groups who defend obscene movies. There are laws and courts, he reminded them, to take action against obscenity. "Why, therefore," he asked, "are there people who in the name of civil liberties, defend the showing in theaters, the advertisement to the public, and the open sale of what is plainly obscene?"

He asked the lawyers whether it is true that immorality is such a vague term that in legal practice it is undefinable. "We talk about teen-age crime problems," he said, "and yet we tolerate these things. When these things are defended in the name of civil liberties, we have departed from our own jurisprudence."

He declared it imperative that sane, sound jurists speak out louder in defining immorality. "Liberty does not mean," he said, "that civil authorities have no power to forbid the actions of individuals who are acting against public welfare."

On the eighth of May, 1954, he openly deplored the dearth of good Catholic literature, and recommended as an offset that Catholic high schools and colleges place greater emphasis on the liberal arts and on developing creative talent.

Three days later, on May 11, the Cardinal directed his attention to quite a different matter, one which called forth only words of praise. It was the teen-agers for a change who were having a campaign, an ambitious drive for modesty, aimed at influencing manufacturers and designers of clothing to provide modest but becoming clothes, especially for teen-age girls. They named the movement: Supply the Demand for the Supply. They were sufficiently successful to be able to hold a fashion show at one of the Chicago hotels, featuring garments designed especially for S.D.S.

This effort did not escape the Cardinal's watchful eyes, nor was he found wanting in commenting upon it. "I am intensely interested," he said, "in having our girls form a right conscience in matters of this kind, and in creating a demand for decent clothing." Later in the year he was to have more to say on the subject of woman's dress.

XXXVI

IT WAS the month of May, 1954. It was the Marian Year and the month of Pius X who, before its end, would be raised to the altars as a saint. It was also time for the Cardinal to go to Rome again. Catholic Chicago would demonstrate its respect for this year of our Lady. Of its 1,983,030 Catholics a quarter of a million would throng into Soldiers' Field on September 8, to participate in a ceremony in her honor. The 9377 nuns of Chicago all had plans for some special tribute of devotion. The Cardinal knew that this fervor would not abate in his absence; for he understood his flock. He was convinced that they would never disappoint him and that he could guide them in spirit, even from afar.

Shortly before his departure he addressed the Catholic Press Association at their annual convention banquet, calling attention to the importance and responsibility of the Catholic press, emphasizing the fact that in countries where atheistic communism has seized control, one of their first efforts is to strangle the Catholic press. Again he stressed the fact that it is not enough for us to teach our children. There is need for adult education, and although we have set up study clubs, forums, and the like, the principal medium for this purpose, apart from the teaching in the churches, is our Catholic press.

He indicated that the convention would face many problems. New techniques have come into journalism and popular writing and since some of them are good, the Catholic press must use them to the fullest extent possible. Its work is to comment, in the light of our faith, on many problems of the time which have a deep moral and religious significance. "You will not become great," said the Cardinal, "because of your mere economic news and comments, nor because of your sports pages nor because of your comics. Your greatness must come from your fidelity in printing Catholic truth and Catholic news and presenting it to your readers."

As for the freedom of the press he maintained that though it is a special blessing in our country, the press is responsible for this very freedom; for the meaning of freedom itself is the freedom to do what is right. He was, however, far from advocating rigidity and identity of opinion on public questions. Honest differences and a variety of opinions will exist, and these must be reflected in our press; but there is a limit beyond which, in the name of freedom, the press cannot go.

"Is it the right," the Cardinal asked, "of a free press to tell the story of ugly happenings in lurid language? Is it the right of a free press to advertise the obscene? Is it the right of a free press to exceed the norms of propriety in picturing and telling of sex? . . . It is commonplace to pick up a newspaper today and to read the expression of honest indignation at the behavior of some public servants and other men, who should be an example in the community, and then to turn the pages and find in that same issue pictures and advertisements which certainly do not reflect a sense of responsibility on the part of the press."

The Cardinal's position on the subject of the press was no uncertain one, and his views were the result of thinking things through. He asked of the press a keener awareness of the responsibility which its freedom imposes upon it. In face of the fact that the press reflects the life of its period he took an affirmative stand in asserting that the press helps to make the life of the day and has the power of molding this life aright. Far from merely reflecting the bad things of the times, it will be strong enough, if aware of its social duty, to make the bad things right and to give us a better day.

In alluding more specifically to the Catholic press the Cardinal said that we do not want to make every statement, even in the so-called diocesan paper, an authoritative one. We should leave great liberty to the expression of opinions on debatable matters and the Catholic press would be more effective if it engaged a little more in controversy on these subjects. A more daring discussion of the debatable problems of our times would certainly arouse greater interest on the part of the reading public. "As long as the Catholic press acts in the light of the teaching of the Church," the Cardinal emphatically declared, "and faithfully presents that teaching, we certainly do not even desire an unfortunate uniformity."

By this, of course, he did not mean that the Catholic press should engage in partisan politics, an activity which he considered would be a great mistake. It should, however, concern itself with the theater problem in all its phases and take a firm stand against the exhibition of the obscene even when at the end of a story or play some sort of applause is given to virtue. The duty of pointing out the danger to morals always remains. "We are living in a changed world," said the Cardinal, "and it is not enough merely to call upon police power after the damage is done."

He insisted that the same opinion must be taken with regard to books, some of which are written by Catholics. Book reviews must give to the people the information that they expect, endorsing what is good and never being too cowardly to point out what is bad, or what may be an occasion of sin.

As was usual with him, the Cardinal did not call attention to an evil without suggesting its remedy. We must do more to provide healthy recreation with the best modern techniques, for our people. We need more gifted writers, and dramatic talent of the highest sort. This will come to a great extent when we support the right Catholic literature and help authors and publishers in spreading it. And here is the opportunity for powerful work on the part of the Catholic press.

He believed "that complacency in a newspaper or publishing office is stagnancy. . . . A holy dissatisfaction with what we are doing is a postulate for progress in our work. . . ."

XXXVII

"COME back, come back to Rome!" The unforgettable call echoed again through the consciousness of Cardinal Stritch. He had answered it many times. Fresh and vibrant it came this Marian Year, as never before since the day when he heard it first in the ringing voice of Pius X. This time it came, as it were, from heaven, from a saint soon to be, and whom the Cardinal had canonized in his heart long ago.

Since his ordination Pius X had been his ideal, and the forthcoming canonization was like a great affirmation of all that Pius X stood for, all that he had meant to him personally. "You will perhaps not see this poor old Pope," he had said. Indeed he would see him now, and often during his stay in Rome, lying in peace below one of the altar tables of St. Peter's where Mass upon Mass would be offered, where the multitudes would crowd about him to pray, to look upon him, to receive Holy Communion. Two tall candles were always burning beside him while the stately guards of St. Peter's kept watch.

For the second time a canonization took place out of doors because of expected throngs: that of St. Pius X followed the pattern of the canonization ceremony for the little Italian girl, St. Maria Goretti. Once more the universal Church, the Church in action, seemed visible while the long procession passed up the outer stairs of St. Peter's. It must have been a joy beyond the power of words for the Cardinal to hear Pius XII proclaim Pius X a saint, and to see unveiled, high upon the façade of St. Peter's, the face that he knew, that had looked upon him with such paternal kindness.

In addition to paying homage to Mary at some of her numerous shrines and to St. Pius X, the Cardinal took upon himself a third duty of loyalty. Not far from Rome, along the sea, lies the little town of Nettuno with its beachhead Anzio, a name that will linger sadly in the memory of many Americans of this generation. To the cemetery at Nettuno the Cardinal went in the name of the bereft Americans who could not come to kneel at the graves of their dead. The Cardinal knelt among the rows of simple crosses and prayed for those young men who, far from home, had met life's ultimate fulfillment.

On May 31 a little group of Czech and Slovak priests and seminarians took advantage of the Cardinal's presence in Rome to give him a reception at the Nepomucene Bohemian College. The seventeen seminarians and five priests, all refugees from behind the Iron Curtain, who had escaped from Red Czechoslovakia in order to pursue their studies in Rome, wished, through His Eminence, to thank the Catholics of the United States for helping them. Some were shot at and a few were wounded while trying to escape. They were now preparing for the priesthood with the hope that eventually they might return to their country. Cardinal Stritch had befriended these young men and procured help for them through their Czech and Slovak friends in the United States. The National Alliance of Czech Catholics and the Slovak Catholic Federation of America have continued this assistance.

"We're proud of you and we want you to know it" Cardinal Stritch told them, "and to know that we are sure you will win through, one day." Archbishop Hoban of Cleveland and his auxiliary, Bishop Krol, with Father Pekarik of Emmaus, Pennsylvania, vice-president of the Slovak Catholic Federation of America were with the Cardinal at this reception.

XXXVIII

UNDER the inspiration of the feast of SS. Peter and Paul, the Cardinal addressed the clergy and the laity of his archdiocese in 1954, through a pastoral describing fully the position of the Church with regard to the participation of Catholics in interfaith meetings seeking church unity. After explaining the primacy of Peter and all that it implies, he made it clear that unity of faith can be attained only by the submission of the individual mind to the voice of God speaking through the Church and particularly through the visible head of the Church, the Vicar of Christ, the Pope.

Since many religious-minded men, deploring the divisions existing among them, gather into organizations and hold conventions for the purpose of establishing unity among Christian churches, a question naturally arises as to the attitude of the Church toward these activities. The answer is that the Church does not allow her children to participate in any conferences based on the false assumption that Roman Catholics also are still searching for the truth of Christ. To do so would be tantamount to an admission that she is but one of the many forms in which the true Church of Christ may or may not exist, that she does not preserve in herself the unity of faith, government, and worship willed by our Lord for His Church, that she does not know the true nature of that unity and of those other God-given properties by which she is distinguished not only as the one but also as the holy, catholic, and apostolic Church founded by Christ. This admission she can never make.

The Cardinal pointed out that the Church by all means desires unity, but only the unity established in her by Jesus Christ, not one that is forged according to fallible human concepts. She longs, prays, and makes every effort to bring Christ's other sheep into His fold; but she remains mindful of her duty to Christ to preserve the deposit of Faith confided to her, intact. To the objection that corruption in the Church caused some of its members to break away from her, the fact that the Church in the sixteenth century believed and taught nothing that was not believed and taught in the first and second centuries is a sufficient reply.

He thus has given an unequivocal statement of the position of the Church with regard to a subject that to some might appear controversial; but he has based his utterances on principles that are immutable and not in the least open to private opinion. He urged Catholics to show forth in their daily lives the holiness of the Church and to let their fellow citizens who are not of the household of the Faith see in them a shining example of Christian charity which embraces all men in the love of God.

The pastoral ends as it began, on the note of SS. Peter and Paul: "We desire, dear sons and daughters in Christ, that you pray fervently to SS. Peter and Paul. Pray for yourselves and pray for our separated brothers that they may come to know the Church of Christ and that they may be given the grace to find peace and joy in it. In this Marian Year, when you are fervently praying to our Blessed Lady the Mother of God, remember your brothers and ask our Blessed Lady to bring them into the unity of the Church. . . ."

XXXIX

PERHAPS the Cardinal's pastoral may best be evaluated by its effect upon someone representative of those vitally involved in it, the "separated brethren" for whom the head of the World Brotherhood organization may be regarded as a fitting spokesman. This society, with its European office in Geneva, Switzerland, characterizes itself as an international organization of religiously motivated citizens working for social justice and international understanding.

According to a statement from its president, Dr. Everett Clinchy, the World Brotherhood understood the doctrinal impossibility of Catholics discussing matters of revealed religion involved in any consideration of church unity. "Certainly in matters of doctrine and dogma there can be no compromises," Dr. Clinchy said. "The notion that all religions are equally valid, the idea that all churches are equally true, implies an indifferentism which the World Brotherhood and the American National Conference of Christians and Jews, formally disavow. . . .

"Cardinal Stritch's call for the civic collaboration of all men of goodwill, particularly those who 'worship the living God,' for the solution of pressing social problems, is applauded by World Brotherhood."

In addition to being president of World Brotherhood, Dr. Clinchy was for 25 years executive director of the National Conference of Christians and Jews. He says further: "My understanding is that the Canon Law dictates that in matters of revelation there can be no public debate, and in worship no cooperation with non-

Catholics; in matters of the natural law, which includes the Fatherhood of God and the brotherhood of man as convictions reached by reason, there can be cooperation with non-Catholics in the civic realm. This is fair and clear — certainly the plea of Pope Pius XII for cooperation among all men of goodwill in this time of mutual danger from atheistic materialism sustains the call of Cardinal Stritch for cooperation among all citizens to establish righteousness, incorruptible integrity, and faith in God throughout the world."

Dr. Clinchy deplored the confusion of collaboration for concrete temporal goals of social progress, interracial justice, and international understanding, with movements for the union of religions. "The objectives are distinct," he declared. "The goals are separate, and neither ideal is served by mixing the methods. There are enough tasks, it would certainly seem, on which religiously-minded men can work together in these days when the very future of a moral civilization is at stake, without compromising cherished dogmatic beliefs. . . .

"I view the Cardinal's statement as constructive, affirmative, and a healthy clarification for both Protestants and Catholics. Personally I never could understand why people had to belong to the same church (nor discuss why they didn't) before being able to work together as citizens to improve housing conditions, to remove prejudices from text-books, or to obtain justice for minority groups."

The half-dozen leaders in the community, when the Cardinal took a stand in Chicago against objectionable literature, were not as understanding of his attitude as Dr. Clinchy proved himself to be. This disclosed itself in mid-October, 1954, during a short stay in Memphis where the Cardinal was visiting a family of old friends after dedicating churches in Ripley and in Covington. As usual, he had a question to discuss and a message to give. This time it was on the subject of literature and he asserted that the answer to the problem of vile literature is a courageous public campaign to inform the people of the evils of the situation.

"Once they are informed," he said, "then will come that great force of public conscience against this thing, and, quite naturally, we'll get the right sort of legislation.

"We have legislation against the sale of narcotics and we have statutes and laws against public obscenity," he declared hopefully. He explained that some years ago he was forced to take action against objectionable literature in the Chicago Archdiocese. Realizing that too many fine adults simply had no idea of what was going on and were consequently unaware of the degree and extent of vile literature, he called in half a dozen leaders in the community and asked for their co-operation in the projected drive.

"During our conversation," the Cardinal continued, "it was evident that the men thought I was overstating the facts. However, they agreed at their expense to engage an investigator.

"When this expert investigator made his report, the men were horrified."

The Cardinal gave proof of understanding facts equally well when, in a strongly worded pastoral, he denounced the present-day dress of women as shocking and immoral. "Modesty," he wrote, "is that virtue which stands guard over the path which may lead to a violation of chastity." He asserted furthermore that the fashions and manners of dress today reflect the denial of the "God-given function of sex and its moral responsibilities."

"Comfort" and "health" reasons he called "poor excuses" and maintained that they do not justify indecent exposure of the body. "Very many safeguards which the Church threw around young girls and matrons, have disappeared in our society. There has been unconventional comradeship between the sexes in our youth, which has brought about dangers which must be recognized and avoided."

The call to follow the example of the Blessed Virgin was the Cardinal's final exhortation of the Marian Year to the almost 2,000,000 Catholics of his archdiocese.

XL

"HAVE you got any money?" the Cardinal asked his Jesuit companion while walking home from the Cathedral one evening. Smiling, the Jesuit dug into his pocket. "I have a vow of poverty," he said. "I'm afraid I haven't very much." "And I'm afraid I need a haircut," replied the Cardinal, enjoying the situation enormously. The Jesuit's hand returned into the open. "I have three dollars and forty cents." "Good!" the Cardinal exclaimed. "Give me the three dollars and you keep the forty cents."

In the light of the Cardinal's almost continuous need of a haircut, it is doubly delightful to find that the civic achievement award for 1955, given to him on April 3 for "outstanding contribution to the cause of interracial justice," was the award of the Journeymen Barbers Local 939 of American Federation of Labor. In announcing the award, special emphasis was placed upon the Cardinal's authorization for the establishment of the Catholic Interracial Council of Chicago in 1946. The Council was declared "one of the outstanding organizations in Chicago, working for better human relations and interracial justice."

With the presentation of the award came a message from Mr. George Meany, president of the American Federation of Labor, declaring Cardinal Stritch a "champion of the workingman and a neighbor of all."

In accepting the award, Cardinal Stritch declared that it was given him as "a symbol of how Christian principles have advanced the cause of labor."

The union in its testimonial pledged itself "each in his own

128

humble way, to put into practice the principles you have so ably exemplified."

This ceremony took place at the Morrison Hotel, Chicago, before a group of labor leaders. The Cardinal's attitude toward labor and the interracial question needs no further comment. Those affected by it are the better judges.

More and more, it seems, during this second decade of his regime in Chicago, the Cardinal was called upon to speak in public. Those about him feared many a time that he was overtaxing his strength; but he admitted no fatigue and gave the whole of himself to each separate thing that made its demands upon him. Some said that he was unable to relax and he agreed that it might be true; but he declared himself as beyond learning new ways and continued blithely to lend himself to the unending variety of claims upon his attention. He had the ability, fortunately, to sleep quickly for a few minutes and to wake up refreshed.

On June 7, 1955, he had occasion to express some of his ideas on architecture when he spoke at the dedication of the new modernistic Church of Christ the King which, at a cost of $750,000, had been erected in suburban Beverly Hills. To those who favored the older, traditional forms of church architecture, this ultramodern edifice was a challenge. The Cardinal rose to it with comments that illustrated his breadth of viewpoint as well as of taste.

Sacred art, he said, whether new or old, must help "lift man's heart and mind to Almighty God," and in the construction of a church, if the effect of sacredness is borne out despite the appearance of the edifice, the traditional lines of church construction are followed. "But unless the builder is careful, it can turn out a barn."

In general the Cardinal was willing to experiment; but to experiment safely. He never wanted to run any risk of compromising the Church in things too experimental. With regard to the newer version of Scripture, he would say almost apologetically: "I am so accustomed to the old Douay version." And from it he could quote voluminously from memory.

In this same month of June the Cardinal spoke at a one-day

institute of social work at Loyola University in Lewis Towers. Enrollment for social work in the universities and colleges of the United States had dropped 30 per cent during the past few years, despite the increased need for social workers. The Cardinal attributed this to public disappointment in the work of the schools in this field and called upon the social workers of the nation to be more human and less autocratic.

He told the 120 workers in Catholic Charities from Illinois, Indiana, and Wisconsin that all social workers must approach their jobs with humility. Such an attitude, he explained, can reverse the "difficult situation."

Later in the year he was advocating a more liberal and reasonable refugee relief program on the part of the United States. He had gone to Cleveland to participate in the celebration commemorating the centenary of the birth of Father Stephen Furdek, Slovak immigrant priest who is honored as the founder of the First Catholic Slovak Union. Cardinal Stritch told the N.C.W.C. News Service that he was happy to pay this tribute to Father Furdek, "to express my admiration and my appreciation of his work, and of the contribution made by him and his people to our Church and our nation."

He thereupon advocated a more liberal policy in connection with the Refugee Relief Act under which some 214,000 refugees were eligible for admission to this country by December 31, 1956. He believed that the same kind of policy should be extended to the United States immigration laws, in order to help these people. "A policy of closing the door too tight against admission of these refugees who are exiled from their own lands to escape tyranny," the Cardinal said, "is not in keeping with our tradition and is not aimed at the best interests of our country.

"History shows what immigration has done to make us a great people. We must not make the mistake in these days of closing our doors tight against admitting into our country many of these poor refugees scattered over other lands who are in suffering and want, and need us as we need them."

As the Cardinal's heart went out to suffering nations, so it was moved at the sorrow of individuals. He was not too busy to send a telegram of sympathy to the parents of three young boys who were found murdered in one of the forest preserves of Chicago.

"I beg Almighty God," the telegram said, "and pray that out of this tragedy there will come a better public conscience for the protection of our youth."

Another example of his interest in the sorrows and the joys of individuals was his attendance at a birthday party at Mercy Hospital for the Andrews twins who were one year old and were the first pair of babies to survive a delicate operation separating their two heads.

"We're all very grateful to our doctors, nurses and Sisters for the expert care they have given the children," he said. "We're glad to be here to congratulate them and their parents on their first birthday and hope they have many more happy ones." One is reminded of St. Paul's "All things to all men."

We may draw a little further upon St. Paul to illustrate how a man in his inner attitudes may be closely akin to someone who lived centuries before him, although the modes of expression may vary with the respective ages in which they lived. St. Paul could descend from the inspired heights of preaching to the Greeks, to being a tentmaker, and Cardinal Stritch could step down from his archepiscopal dignity to being a collector of jeeps for missionary work in Bolivia. The little story began in Rome when the Cardinal readily gave permission that one of his priests be taken to serve the Church in the Secretariate of State. This priest later became secretary to the papal nuncio in La Paz, Bolivia. When he attended the Thirty-Sixth International Eucharistic Congress in July, 1955, in Rio de Janeiro he met Cardinal Stritch, who invited him to join his party.

While discussing the conditions of the Church in Bolivia, the Cardinal inquired as to the principal need in the missionary work there. "The great need is for jeeps," the priest said. "There is no way of reaching many of the people in remote regions. With the help of jeeps one might penetrate to these areas." The Cardinal listened intently in the meantime, with his customary gesture when in thought, taking a firm hold of his nose.

"How many would you need?" he asked. "Twenty or twenty-five would be of enormous help," the priest replied.

When the Cardinal returned to Chicago the thought that a priest should be held back in his missionary work for want of jeeps disturbed him; and he had to do something about it. Throughout the summer at Clearwater Lake he kept at it until people were asking: "What's the idea, the Cardinal running around getting jeeps?" By the end of the summer he had them.

The next need to be supplied in Bolivia was a radio station that the Church might broadcast her message to the people in the mountains. Another was money for the building of a seminary. The Cardinal's visit to Rio did not end with the Eucharistic Congress. His concern for the Church was not bounded by his own archdiocese. To him the needs of the Church were of vital import whether in Rome, in Chicago, or in the wilds of Bolivia.

XLI

"THERE are a lot of people today who amount to something because they were newspaper boys" the Cardinal announced at the annual luncheon of the archdiocesan newspaper, the *New World*, at the Sheraton-Blackstone Hotel. Then with a twinkle of mischief he added: "In fact I was one, too."

He told them that when he was a boy in Nashville, he had a

60-paper route. The students, who had made such a success of their campaign for the New World and had come to receive their prizes, relished this information. Twenty of them, the Cardinal admitted, had sold him a subscription, so he was now receiving twenty copies of the paper.

If he was proud of his newspaper boys, he had occasion to be proud also of the magnificent gathering of guests who came to attend his charity dinner on the evening of November 14, 1955. Their contribution this year amounted to $270,000. "You have opened your hearts," he told them.

It was the sixth time since 1949 that the great ballroom of the Conrad Hilton Hotel was aglow with light and color for its more than one thousand guests; but on this particular evening a touch of silver threaded the usual red of the decorations, for it was twenty-five years since the Cardinal had been raised to the rank of archbishop. He was the genial host as always; but something serious was on his mind. A movement was afoot to make taxpayers assume all charities and with vigor he rose to denounce it: "They are trying to substitute a State charity. If they do this here, we may as well tear down the Stars and Stripes."

The Cardinal emphasized the fact that when man has a sense of responsibility to God, he will take care of his social obligations; but when he substitutes the State for God, we have tragedy. Happily there was no tragedy in the Cardinal's charity. The generous proceeds of the dinner went to meet the operating deficit of the Stritch College of Medicine at Loyola University as before, and to make provision for the Lewis Maternity Hospital.

Anniversaries followed one another closely for the Cardinal. Only a few months after the epochal charity banquet, on February 20, 1956, the Conrad Hilton Hotel was the scene of another festivity when three thousand fourth-degree Knights of Columbus celebrated his tenth anniversary as cardinal with what the Master Knight described as "the largest all-male dinner ever held in a hotel in the United States." When the Cardinal rose to speak the Knights in mighty chorus sang: Happy Anniversary to Cardinal Stritch!"

With this great audience of men before him the Cardinal could not miss his chance to tell them: "Today's greatest danger is secularism — doing things without God."

Bishop Zuroweste of Belleville, Illinois, state chaplain of the Knights of Columbus, in congratulating Cardinal Stritch, became reminiscent. "Ten years ago," he said, "a humble, devout man, a great Churchman, Archbishop Stritch, knelt before Pope Pius XII to receive the Red Hat. That was a magnificent picture of two great Shepherds of the Church together."

The Cardinal, it seems, was neither flattered nor embarrassed by the eulogies and awards that were heaped upon him. For himself he simply did not exist. He had submerged his own personality long ago into that of the priest, losing it in the wide reaches of the Church that he loved. Consequently the appreciation so unstintingly given him beat upon the surface of his life, never finding its way into his soul to do him harm.

In the meantime all was not well in Europe. Hungary was entering upon her agony and the shadow of it lay upon the spirit of the Cardinal at the charity banquet of 1956 at the Conrad Hilton Hotel. "Genghis Khan was an admirable person compared with what we see before us today," he told his guests. "In Hungary, the land of St. Stephen, the face of the beast is exposed before the world. Only yesterday, there were some willing to accept communism's smile — to call it 'just another phenomenon in world evolution.' . . . Today they know better."

Of America's role in this time of crisis, the Cardinal said: "We are proud of the Stars and Stripes. They are a beacon of peace, a defender of right, and a proclamation to the world that we never will suffer a debasing of our freedoms."

The Cardinal himself was able to stand for America in her role of mercy when from overseas a plane, heavily laden with Hungarian refugees, arrived in Chicago. At the airport he was waiting, and for many men, women, and children crowding down the narrow stairway, his smile of welcome was the first impression of America, and a sense of security lay warm in the clasp of his hand. Nor did his part in their lives end with this first gracious gesture. His ever ready charity remained at hand to help them as far as possible in finding homes, work, or the means to travel to some farther destination.

XLII

"HIS EMINENCE is busy," said the master of ceremonies at one of the numerous functions that the Cardinal attended. The master of ceremonies was trying to protect the Cardinal from the persistence of some Knights of Columbus who wanted him to come aside that they might take his picture. He noticed the little scene, and unwilling as he always was to disappoint anyone, he settled the matter at once.

"I'm not busy," he said in his leisurely way. "I'll go with you." And he did. Beyond the reach of the half-accusing and half-patient eye of the master of ceremonies, he took time for another little interruption when he saw a woman surrounded by a brood of small children, patted her on the shoulder, and told her: "You're doing fine work."

"You are doing fine work." This precisely is the comment that, under the guise of awards and testimonials, was coming to the Cardinal from various directions. On August 6, 1956, he received an award from the George Washington Carver Memorial Institute for "bettering race relations and the cause of brotherhood." This time he was spared a banquet. The presentation was made at the Chancery by a group including the president of the Institute. The simple fact that lay at the base of all his work for interracial amity constituted the essence of his reply: "There is no distinction of race under the Fatherhood of God."

In the meantime, concerned as he was with the major dangers threatening the peace of the world or the souls of men, the Cardinal was equally solicitous about so everyday a menace to human safety as reckless driving. This danger affected him so strongly that he wrote a pastoral letter calling attention to the moral responsibility of motorists. "Reckless driving, speeding, and disobeying traffic regulations," he said, "are sins." He asked that young people especially, be instructed on the "important moral obligation of safe driving, and pointed out that the Pope had recently found it necessary to enlighten all men on this moral responsibility of motorists.

The last major public event at which the Cardinal spoke toward the close of the year 1956, was the dedication of the $200,000 Alumni Hall of De Paul University of which he was chancellor. The hall is a combination auditorium and physical-education building. On this occasion the Cardinal had some significant things to say on the subject of education, always one of his primary interests. His opening statement was:

"One of the great tragedies of the modern educational system," he said, "is that we have so many uneducated graduates of institutions of higher learning. . . . Too many have failed to develop the intelligence to reach out for the truth. . . . There are only a few to whom we are indebted for the advances made in the field of natural sciences."

He held that the purpose of education is to develop the whole man. For this reason he believed a good physical education important in the formation of good students. This does not, however, include "overestimation of the importance of victory of athletic teams in competition with other schools" or "the operating of a farm for training professional athletes."

He held that schools "which sacrifice accepted standards in order to provide more athletes for better competition" have the wrong outlook. He emphasized this point also when speaking to the Midwest secondary school unit of the National Catholic Educational Association on April 4, 1957. "There is something wrong," he said, "when athletic prowess is prized above intellectual achievement." He then added a further consideration which has perhaps more bearing upon secondary education: "We find in recreation, even where we should not find it, a surrender of the dignity of the human person. It cannot be passed over by saying it's all in youth. In the development of the Christian person there can be no surrender."

At the same occasion he warned educators against "Mass action, mass thinking and mass psychology in great urban industrial centers," and advised strongly against adopting "standards from sources not ultimately concerned in human welfare, but in making money." In few words, precisely to the point, the Cardinal also outlined plans for expanded school facilities in the archdiocese. The growth of the Catholic population of Chicago which was expected to pass the two million mark by the end of 1957, had brought its problems, notably where schools were concerned. The Cardinal estimated that by 1962 high school facilities will have been expanded sufficiently to handle 80 per cent of the students graduating from parochial elementary schools. "When 80 per cent capacity is achieved in 1962," said the Cardinal, "then the next step, full capacity, will be possible." For the administrator of the Archdiocese of Chicago there was no standing still.

Shortly after the opening of the year 1957 Cardinal Stritch received the highest decoration that Italy gives, the Grand Cross of Merit "In recognition of the many wonderful things he has done for Italy and for the Italian community of the archdiocese." The Italian ambassador to the United States made the presentation on January 13 at a dinner which approximately 1500 people attended, including the governor of Illinois, the mayor of Chicago, and two state senators from Illinois.

During the ambassador's visit the Cardinal and he were having a conversation in Italian when newspaper photographers interrupted them, wishing to take their pictures. The Cardinal made a comment in Italian and they both laughed. According to a translation by someone close at hand, the Cardinal had remarked that he hoped when these good men get to heaven, that they would not have their camera machines with them.

Decorations and honors followed apace. The Knights of Malta presented him with their medal Pro-Hungaria in token of the help he had given to Hungarian exiles, and on March 14 he was inducted as honorary member of Phi Kappa fraternity in a ceremony at his residence. It was worth more than a medal of honor to him, however, to receive the report of Father Fitzgerald, the Paulist pastor of Old St. Mary's, whom he had encouraged some years previous, in the employment of correspondence-school techniques for the studying of the Catholic religion. With every year this home-study course under the program of the Confraternity of Christian Doctrine had met with more response. The first year 2000 Chicagoans had responded to the advertisement and during the year 1956 there were 6248 replies. "Modern methods of spreading the faith are expensive," said Father Fitzgerald. "But when one considers that each convert's soul is priceless, the cost of advertising seems pretty reasonable to us."

At a Mass in the Cathedral on April 29, 1957, at which the Cardinal preached the sermon, his interest in youth reached out beyond their educational facilities with which he had so recently been occupied. The Mass was being offered in celebration of the thirtieth anniversary of the Chicago Inter-Student Council for Catholic Action, the so-called CISCA. The 2000 high school boys and girls who attended represented some 75,000 students of 95 parochial high schools of the archdiocese.

Speaking on the dignity of youth, the Cardinal said: "This dignity does not come in dress or other things. It is by Christ's ideals that we must recapture the true spirit of youth. It is for you today to participate with me in the apostolate of the archdiocese . . . make this apostolate rich in action and sanctity of life."

Meanwhile the Cardinal wrote a pastoral condemning the practice of business-as-usual on Sunday, ruling out, thereby, all unnecessary Sunday business activity.

The Cardinal takes up the matter of Sunday business by asking and answering a number of questions. The general principles, however, are that a Catholic businessman may not conduct his business on Sundays, and Catholics may not make purchases on Sunday.

XLIII

"AGATHA, there's a long distance call for you from Chicago," said the nurse in a Detroit hospital, plugging in a telephone and holding it for the Negro woman who could scarcely turn her head. Her operation had been so serious that she had received the Last Sacraments on that very day. "Hello Aggie," a soft southern voice that she knew came over the wire. It was Cardinal Stritch calling from Chicago to inquire how she was getting along.

She was Agatha Hodge who was the first Negro baby that he had baptized. At that very moment the rosary which he gave her for her first Holy Communion was wound about her fingers. He had never lost track of her; but had always written on special occasions and she had saved all the letters. When, after encouraging her and assuring her of prayers, the voice from Chicago said, "Good-by and God bless you," the nurse hung up the receiver; but the glow did not leave Agatha's eyes and a spark of life came back into her face. "She'll live," the nurse said to herself as she left the room.

Agatha did live, and she loved to tell the story of that long, faithful friendship. Her mother had worked for the Stritch family in Nashville and when the Cardinal shortly after his return from

Rome was assigned to Memphis, she went as rectory housekeeper and to keep an eye on "her family" as she expressed it. Agatha recalled a time when her mother had gotten into some financial trouble over an investment and that it was Father Stritch, "even then," as she said, "an expert handler of finances," who came to the rescue. Within a few hours he had the whole matter straightened out. Since then he had been a friend and adviser. This began in 1911 or shortly thereafter. It was now the year 1956.

The Cardinal's kindly attitude toward Negroes did not confine itself to interracial councils. He demonstrated a real affection for them on numerous occasions. One day during his earlier years in Chicago his secretary met a Negro who inquired with great concern about the Cardinal. He had played with "Sammy," he said, as a little boy in Nashville. When the secretary alluded to His Eminence, the Negro said that to him he was always Sammy. He had never called him anything else. He had not ventured to visit the Cardinal because of his high position; but he did want to send him a greeting.

When the secretary mentioned the incident at dinner that evening the Cardinal was overjoyed. As soon as the meal ended he rose from the table. "Let us go to him at once," he said.

The Cardinal often enjoyed making unexpected visits. One sunny afternoon the pastor of a North Side parish of Chicago, where a large building project was in progress, saw a black Cadillac standing in front of the rectory. No one was in it; but the figure 1 stood out on its license plate and this could belong only to one person. For years no one but the Archbishop of Chicago had carried that license number.

The pastor, just returning home, saw it and for a moment was rooted to the spot. The Cardinal had never come unannounced. He was not waiting in the rectory. What could this possibly mean? Just then he caught a glimpse of William Gibbons, the chauffeur, taking a leisurely walk on the other side of the street. The latter saw the pastor's puzzled face and pointed to the unfinished building. The monsignor crossed over to the gymnasium-to-be and there he found the Cardinal.

"But, Your Eminence," he exclaimed with a voice filled with apologies. "If I had only known of your coming, I might have been here to receive you." The Cardinal smiled a roguish smile as he said: "I wanted to see what I wanted to look at, not what you wanted to show me."

This was the third time that Samuel Stritch had given this particular monsignor a surprise. On the first occasion it was the Bishop of Toledo who won his heart. The pastor was a very young priest at the time. It was Mother's Day, and he was on duty at the Mission of the Holy Cross of which Monsignor Kiley was the head, when the extremely youthful Bishop of Toledo came to have a look at the mission. Monsignor Kiley, later archbishop of Milwaukee, was in his working clothes.

The young priest was at the desk alone when the Bishop came in. "What are you doing here on Mother's Day?" he asked with a warm smile. The young priest explained that he was on duty. The Bishop looked sympathetic, but unconvinced. "You go home to your mother," he said. "I just want to look around a bit and I'll find Monsignor Kiley." It was impossible not to do as the Bishop said, the Monsignor related many years after the incident; for he asked it as though it were a favor.

Years later, when the erstwhile Bishop of Toledo and Archbishop of Milwaukee had become Archbishop of Chicago and the young priest of Mother's Day was the pastor of a parish composed largely of miserable hovels in an industrial section to the south of Chicago, the Archbishop came for a visit. He was appalled at the poverty of the parochial buildings. "Do you mean to tell me," he said, "that my priests and 400 children in the school have to live in such conditions? They must be improved, whether you can pay for it or not." This was but one of many examples where the Cardinal entered with wholehearted generosity into the problems of a parish and gave the required financial aid.

In 1957 from the first of May to the fifth, the Catholic Commission on Intellectual and Cultural affairs held their convention in

Chicago and invited the Cardinal to speak. On subject matter most congenial to him, he gave fullness of expression to his ideas on civilization, culture, and scholarship, with their ultimate reference to Divine Revelation and to God Himself. The address shows the Cardinal in the process of his thinking. It reveals the great synthesis of his own life, somewhat in the way that Newman's *Idea of a University* reveals the great English Cardinal.

Cardinal Stritch believes that civilization and culture are correlative. Civilization he defines as "perfection in securing the common good," and culture is that ingredient of civilization which gives it its perfection and worth. Although civilization is a collective reality, it is the achievement of the human person. All its norms must therefore come from the postulates of the human person in his social life.

The dignity of the human person and the development of his talents have always been a pivotal point in the Cardinal's thinking. He believes, consequently, that culture inheres in the obligation native to the human person, of perfecting his potentialities. This idea in turn leads to the concept of scholarship and indicates the importance of scholars who have the duty of making society aware of its highest needs. "To belittle the scholar," the Cardinal said, "is to belittle man. To fail in a society to cultivate profound scholarship is failing to make its civilization worthy of a *homo sapiens.*"

It would, however, not be like the Cardinal to stop at this point; for to him *homo sapiens* or a rational being who is a Catholic is the material for a lay apostle, and a profound scholar who is a Catholic has an important place in the lay apostolate. He is perfecting his own person in developing his powers, and doing so in the Catholic way as an offering to God, he is fulfilling the commandment of loving God with his mind and therefore laboring at his own sanctification. Inevitably this gives him a special opportunity to help the Church in bearing witness to Christ. Whether consciously or unconsciously he can become an influence among those who are, as the Cardinal says, "making the Main Streets of tomorrow."

He can demonstrate that the Gospel of Christ answers the questions which every seeker after truth must face. He can supply the evidence that nowhere can the scholar find a more congenial atmosphere than in the Church. In addition to the truths attainable by human reason, he has the truths of Divine Revelation to draw upon, an added light in the strenuous search for truth, a further encouragement in the quest for beauty.

Since in our country the number of intellectuals in the Lay Apostolate is small, the Cardinal suggests two things that must be done to remedy this weakness. He maintains, first of all, that liberal education must be given its proper place. Classrooms must be related more to the development of culture than to the mere making of a living; for even in the training of specialists there is no substitute for liberal education.

Secondly, since our way of life today has tended to make us forget the dignity of the human person, the Catholic educator has an opportunity of tremendous import. Apart from what mere philosophy teaches, he is able to see the human person in the light of the Redemption. Christ died for men, not for humanity, for every human person as an individual. In His Blood we are brothers and as such He calls upon us to unite with Him in carrying on the work of redemption. This thought, if instilled into the minds of Catholic youth, is sufficiently powerful to develop in them the enthusiasm for loving God with their whole minds. This enthusiasm and this love will begin the increase of profound scholars in the Lay Apostolate.

The Cardinal sees reasons for optimism in the fact that many parents, having enjoyed opportunities for higher education, have made homes where culture is fostered. These homes are the key to creating an appreciation for scholarship and a desire in youths to seek it. The Cardinal referred to the Pope's Easter address in which Pius XII praised the advances of science, and he called attention to the numerous ways in which the Holy Father has encouraged scholarship in all fields of learning and research. "To know truth," said the Cardinal, "lifts one up to the Source of Truth. To reach out for beauty brings a better appreciation of the Beauty of God, of which all beauty in nature is but a reflection."

In the midst of a superlatively active life the Cardinal's enthusiasm for scholarship was never in abeyance. Nevertheless it did not cause him to withdraw into a book-lined, soundproof library world. For him scholarship, vital as it is, never stood alone, an end in itself. It was linked creatively with the dignity of human personality, the Lay Apostolate, the life of the Church. He did not address his audience merely as an intellectual speaking to intellectuals. He said instead: "You will begin to wonder where I, a bishop of Holy Church, am leading you. You want to know what the Church has to say to you." Not for a moment did he forget that he was essentially the Churchman, with the inseparable ego not annihilated, but completely immersed in the thing that he loved. He has said: "The lethargic person who does not offer the fullness of his gifts does not love God with his whole mind."

XLIV

TRIXIE, the toy bull, walked solemnly into the dining room one morning in July, 1957, to greet the Cardinal who was glancing at the newspaper over his abstemious breakfast of orange juice and coffee. The toy bull did not frisk about as usual; but returned to the kitchen with its bit of a tail as low as its limited possibilities would allow. Something was not as it had been these years and years. William Gibbons, the chauffeur, had not come into the kitchen this morning, nor yesterday morning, nor the day before.

Though Trixie did not know it, the man who for 28 years had driven the car with Illinois license plate number 1, had retired and gone to Florida. "I'm sorry to leave my job," he had said. "But I asked my boss — pardon me, His Eminence, the Cardinal — to permit me to retire. I wish I was younger and could continue in service. Both Cardinal Stritch and Cardinal Mundelein were the grandest bosses to work for." He pronounced both cardinals "excellent passengers. . . . I used my own judgment in driving. Most of the traveling consisted in taking them to Church functions, the seminary at Mundelein, Ill., and to visit bishops in nearby cities."

We have the chauffeur's word for it that the Cardinal was never a back-seat driver. He wrote the following letter to Mr. Gibbons on his retirement: "I regret losing you, because always you have been so understanding and helpful in my work. At times, you were called upon to make hard sacrifices, but you did it with such gentility that you made my work easier. . . . May God bless you."

The Cardinal, however, would not need his chauffeur for a while. Europe once more was in the offing. He was going to Rome again, the home that never changed, for his *ad limina* visit, and the additional plan was to spend five weeks touring Italy, France, and Ireland.

Italy as always, with the swing of its mountains, its green-garmented valleys, its graceful vineyards, its magnificent old stones and columns, its villages like fortresses on the hillsides, was one long reminiscence. He always enjoyed when possible, going down to Tor de Quinto to see Don Cesare Rodolfi who worked with youth. There he would say Mass, visit the youth center, and, where he saw need, make promises which the business people at home helped him to fulfill.

Rome, however, of which he knew every turn, was the Italian home-coming; and its heart was the Holy Father with whom he had two delightful audiences, an account of which he would bring back to his people in Chicago.

From Italy the Cardinal and his little party: Archbishop O'Brien, Monsignor Hardiman, his secretary, and Father Joseph Egan, S.J., president of the Pontifical Faculty of the seminary at Mundelein, traveled into France. There the tour became a pilgrimage on its way to Lourdes. About Lourdes, also, there is an atmosphere of eternity, with our Lady always waiting in the selfsame place, in the cleft of the rock.

In the afternoon procession the Cardinal had the privilege of carrying the Blessed Sacrament. In all the world there is no procession such as this. With songs of *Hosanna* and prayers for help and healing, the nations of the earth walk together while the sick and the maimed with tense expectancy await the slow approach of the Divine Physician. To the Cardinal with his heart of charity it must have seemed as though stricken humanity were stretched out before him as he passed, stopping, as the custom is, to lift the monstrance in individual blessing over every suffering one. Here, as nowhere else, he could feel that he was dispensing at firsthand the charity of Christ.

Thirty years ago the Bishop of Toledo sat down in the living room of a house in Boleenshere, Ballyheigue, County Kerry, Ireland, and with a look of contentment and a quiet voice said: "This is my goal." He had come to see the crumbling ruins of a school where his grandfather had been principal teacher and where his father had received his first lessons. The Cardinal's grandfather, Thomas Stritch, had come from County Cork and his appointment to the school in Kerry was perhaps the first of the national teacher posts to be established in Ireland. Here Garrett Stritch, the Cardinal's father, was born and now, as cardinal, Samuel Stritch came to see his father's ancestral home at Fernmount, occupied at present by his cousins.

With a heart and a half, as the Irish say, the whole town turned out to greet their distinguished visitor and his party. He had both a liturgical and a civic reception. A dinner was given in his honor and the Irish children danced and sang with exuberance. Many of the Cardinal's relatives are still living in Ireland and a number of them are priests and nuns.

"Hold your Faith," the Cardinal exhorted them. "Be true to your Faith and in these days of much materialism don't forget there is no solution of the world's problems until the world comes to understand, like you do, the dignity of the human person at the foot of the Cross."

The Cardinal was deeply touched by the warm Irish welcome, and with this mood upon him he told the people of Ballyheigue why he had come "home."

"There are times," he said, "when the heart fights with the intellect and makes it difficult to express your innermost thoughts. Today is one of those days for me. I come here among you, the son of a Ballyheigue man, who through no fault of his, more than eighty years ago left Ireland — because he was too Irish.

"I come here today to verify again the picture of Ballyheigue my father gave me when I was a little boy. The day before he died he took me and my next brother — the two youngest in the family — in his arms and . . . told us of his home; he told us of the golden strand, and he told us of the old thatched schoolhouse. He was dreaming, but he painted a picture that always remained in our hearts, and I think both my brother and I had one ambition — to come here and see if this picture was only an exile's dream — or a reality.

"We came and saw that he had not painted half the beauty of the landscape that is here. So I come to you today, not only as this Kerryman's son — the son of this old Ballyheiguer — but a cardinal of Holy Church."

Upon his return to Chicago the Cardinal spoke primarily of the Pope. He reported that His Holiness was "in wonderful health" and "intensely interested in the Church of the United States." He described his two audiences with the Holy Father as highlights of his trip and said also that the Pope "is very grateful for what the Catholics of the United States are doing in giving relief to sufferers in other countries."

He told of economic conditions in Italy and had something to say about the youth of that country. He compared what he observed during this visit with the state of the country in 1946, when he was made cardinal.

"It was just after the war," he declared. "Italy and all of Europe were suffering. Today it is different, especially what I noticed in Italy. The people seem happier, better fed, and looking forward to a good future. The economic conditions have improved greatly. Unemployment, however, is still a problem in Italy.

"I visited several camps of the Italian youngsters. Through the Pope, the bishops' relief agency of our country, and surplus foods of the United States, these youngsters are able to enjoy summer camp life." The Cardinal estimated that the youngsters thus benefited amounted to about one million.

At one of the children's camps the Cardinal praised the work of Monsignor Baldelli, head of the Relief Organization. He learned also that the Catholic Relief Services of the National Catholic Welfare Conference distributes more than one half of the food consumed in these summer camps.

Toward the end of August it was time once more for the annual message to the schools, and the Cardinal re-emphasized his appeal for stronger bonds between home and school. He urged that Home-School Associations be established in every parish, through which, he said: "we hope to realize better in practice, our Catholic teaching that parents are the first educators of their children and that our schools exist and operate to help parents in this arduous task."

He declared it necessary that parents be brought more and more into the school program, "so that they may know more fully our school ideas, purposes, and problems and be more active in the whole education of their children and youths." For the moment all was well with the parish; but since his solicitude was not bounded by archdiocesan limits he found cause for anxiety in the menace of inflation that was hovering over the country. He saw the danger in all its reality, and in his usual way, made an effort to do something about it. He therefore called upon organized labor to take the lead in seeking out the causes of inflation and made his appeal at the September convention of the Illinois State Federation of Labor, urging the delegates to subordinate group interest to the common good.

He gave credit to labor for contributing largely to the progress made in giving economic freedom to millions in our country and cherished the hope that it would correspond to the ideal which the American people have of organized labor. "That ideal," said the Cardinal, "is rooted in something which is common to you and me — for it is my duty and my office to preach to all men the dignity of man, that dignity which the ancient world never saw despite its great philosophers, but which came into the minds of men when our Blessed Saviour died upon the cross for each and every man."

XLV

IT WAS well for the Cardinal that sometimes in the late evening when he was not reading Dante or perhaps some Greek or Latin philosopher, that he would give a little time to watching television or working a crossword puzzle; for in public activities there was no surcease. In his address to 500 jurists at breakfast after the twenty-third annual Red Mass at the Cathedral, he felt in duty bound to speak out against a new proposal advanced by a study group, which he did not name, that certain private immoral acts should not come under the civil law.

He gave warning first of all, against the thought that the preservation of freedom knows no restraints. This he branded as a dangerous error. He maintained furthermore that there are numerous immoral acts which have a definite bearing on the common good and that it would be a sad mistake to exclude these from the prohibition of civil laws. We must hold to our practice of preventing as well as punishing.

This brought the Cardinal's attention to a need for defining the relationship of the sociologist to courts and to lawyers and he asserted that while the sociologist may be helpful, it would be a mistake to substitute sociology for jurisprudence. Apart from the above connection the Cardinal, in a private letter, made the following pertinent comments on sociology:

"In our modern world, in the field of sociology and social studies there is the danger of professionalism. The needs of the poor and the underprivileged are looked upon merely as social problems. The consequence is that those who do this work do not reach down into those whom they are trying to help and see the whole of these persons. . . . All the sociology in the world, all the fine treatises done by learned men will not be of any avail unless all this is done in the reaches of real Christian charity, which penetrate into the very souls of people."

While the Cardinal was turning his attention to schools and parishes, to labor and inflation, to lawyers and sociologists, he became equally interested in hearing a report from one of the doctors of the Stritch Medical School on a cardiovascular project. While he was writing letters and pastorals, speaking, preaching, confirming, and laying cornerstones, another undertaking for the benefit of the Faith was making headway in Chicago. In July, 1957, two months before the publication of the papal encyclical *Miranda Prorsus*, an archdiocesan office for radio and television came into existence. The work of the office is twofold. It creates and promotes programs of a Catholic nature and it provides technical advice and assistance to the stations in the community. This activity is a potent instrument in disseminating Catholic news and information, in arousing interest in the Catholic position, in demonstrating, under the form of drama, the impact of religion on the problems of modern living. Television, furthermore, brought the Cardinal more intimately into the domestic picture. One could see him sitting in his home while answering questions or chatting with an interviewer just as though he were present at the fireside in the homes of his people.

XLVI

"I HOPE you feel fresher than you look," said the Cardinal, looking into the tired eyes of a busy Jesuit who was about to preach a sermon in the Cathedral. Then, with an encouraging smile: "But you're not speaking in your own person. You're speaking in the name of Christ. You'll do well."

"How about walking me to my home?" he asked after services were over. "But you have no bodyguard," the priest said looking around. It was night and the Cardinal was usually given protection when he walked out alone. "I don't need one," the Cardinal said as though he were glad to be free.

He reveled in things intellectual and loved to talk theology. With this priest the conversation would be stimulating and completely to his taste. "Can you tell me the time, Your Eminence?" the priest asked as they approached "the quietest house in the city." "I broke my wrist watch against the marble of the pulpit, this evening." "Come in," the Cardinal urged. "I have many watches. I'll give you one."

Up in his study the Cardinal laid out his array of watches, all of them gifts. Some were of exquisite workmanship, many were valuable. The priest looked them over, admired them, then chose the plainest, cheapest one. The Cardinal looked his approval. "I'm glad that you didn't take one of these," he said indicating the precious ones. "We're priests and I don't think we should be attached to any such things."

Once more, in November, the time was at hand for the annual charity dinner, "the best and the last." This eighth banquet at $250 a plate brought a record attendance of 1150 persons, whom the Cardinal told that they make it possible to continue medical institutions for doctors "who understand the sacredness of human beings." He told them also that by their presence they proved the falsity of the charge that Americans are too materialistic.

Mayor Daley of Chicago expressed his "gratitude to the Cardinal for his great schools, churches, institutions and hospitals, which have helped to make Chicago a great city."

With the coming of Christmas a totally different type of gratitude was expressed to the Cardinal in a completely different way. One hundred needy boys were made happy at Christmas time with new outfits of clothing from which no item was omitted. For the Cardinal, their joy and enthusiasm were sufficient thanks. One of the first in line was a thirteen-year-old who declared emphatically: "I want everything gray, everything to match." Their outbursts of gratitude were an annual joy to the Cardinal, and this was the twenty-fifth year of the tradition.

On New Year's Eve the Cardinal was sitting alone with a volume of Greek in his hands when his secretary passed and stopped to wish him a Happy New Year. Some passage in the Greek tome was apropos at the moment and the Cardinal entered upon an explanation of it. Carried away by his subject he held his listener's attention for two and a half hours. This time he did not even ask, as he had done after an unusually lengthy sermon: "Was I too long?" On one rare occasion, however, he did preach a short sermon. It was a hot July day and he asked: "Did you ever hear me give a short sermon? Listen to this one." He preached for exactly two and a half minutes; but that was in July, not on the thirty-first of December.

XLVII

THE hum of an electric razor had sounded steadily from the Cardinal's quarters one morning in the first week of January, 1958, when suddenly it stopped and clattered to the floor. Surprised, the Cardinal stooped to pick up the razor and could not. His right arm had gone dead and he had not even felt himself dropping the razor.

It was nothing, he told himself. It would pass. It did, and the Cardinal gave it little further thought. The feast of the Epiphany was at hand and to please the Puerto Ricans he would have to attend a banquet. The hair shirt was making itself felt early in the year. A charming gift, however, was his reward. A painting of the Three Kings by a Chicago artist was the symbol of appreciation that he received for his assistance to the 30,000 Puerto Ricans of Chicago.

Since symbols are often profoundly significant, this picture of the Three Kings, the givers of gifts, presented to the Cardinal, tempts the imagination to seek in the three gifts of the Magi, charged with meaning as they are, some symbolic interpretation of the intensity of living and giving that denoted the Cardinal in his essential meaning. So far as the gift of gold was concerned he could almost have said with the Apostles Peter and John: "Silver and gold I have none; but what I have I give thee."

As for the second gift of the Kings as illustrated in the life of the Cardinal, we have not far to seek. If we penetrate to the inner source where paradoxes meet, and ask ourselves what could this secret power be, by which a gentle, self-forgetful personality expresses itself in terms of dynamic activity, the answer will come in the words of the Apocalypse: "and there was given to him much incense." It was this inner incense by which the outer man of action worked and spent himself. While the Cardinal was speaking in many places the language of world affairs, the language of lawyer and labor leader, of medical man and architect, of educator or sociologist, he had the following words to give when he spoke, for instance, to Dominican tertiaries.

"The greatest gift we can give the Church is progress in the supernatural life. . . . Remember, in the mind of St. Dominic what you have undertaken was not just for a particular group, but your undertaking is to contribute something which the Church in this world needs more than anything else — sanctity."

In the third King's gift, the gift of myrrh to Christ as man, one who was to suffer and die, the symbolism is manifest as something that every human being understands; but in the life of the Cardinal it had a special and a personal significance. As he kept Christ the High Priest ever present as the model for his own priesthood, so, in a manner unknown to the world, unsuspected even by many who knew him well, the Cardinal in his hidden austerities imitated also the suffering Christ, and his intimate life could verify the words of the Canticle: "A bundle of myrrh is my Beloved to me."

On the twenty-fifth of February Cardinal Stritch was in Washington to offer the invocation at the Conference on Foreign Aspects of United States National Security, in which both President Eisenhower and former President Truman participated. He was not so much concerned with the honor that it was, as with the opportunity that it provided. Here in the capital of his country, in the presence of its chief executive, he could deliver a message, a message sanctified into a prayer.

In it he alluded to the grave obligation which Divine Providence has placed upon our country of being the protagonist of genuine peace, the unselfish defender of the dignity and rights of the human person. He emphasized the urgency of laboring unceasingly for the organization of international society under just laws which will help the weak and restrain the strong among the nations. He called attention to the duty of sharing our substance prudently with peoples in need. He prayed that God might give us light and strength to enact wisely a program of foreign aid and to administer it in the cause of a genuine world peace.

In conclusion he prayed: "Bless and strengthen our Chief Executive, the President of our country! Give light and wisdom to our congress! Help us to be a people acceptable to Thee. These things humbly we ask of Thee through Jesus Christ our Lord and Saviour, Amen."

XLVIII

"DANNY" the Cardinal exclaimed, while the picture of a well-remembered small boy, a pupil of St. Francis de Sales' School, who had served his Mass in Toledo, flashed into his mind. It was indeed Danny Thomas, prosperous and popular, who was kneeling to kiss his ring. He had come for advice.

Once upon a time when the years were lean for Danny and his course was still uncharted, he lit a candle before the statue of St. Jude, and he promised he would build a shrine in the saint's honor. This he envisioned as a hospital for children, black and white, who were afflicted with hopeless diseases. St. Jude had been propitious. Danny was ready to keep his promise and had come to seek counsel from Cardinal Stritch as to where he should build this hospital.

It did not take the Cardinal long to decide. He suggested Memphis. It was a railroad center. It had become a great medical center. And happily, a little sentiment was not amiss among these practical advantages. Memphis was in the home-state, the Cardinal's beloved Tennessee.

On the first of March the ecclesiastical world was startled by a message which streaked over the Atlantic to tell Cardinal Stritch that the Holy Father had appointed him Pro-Prefect of the Sacred Congregation for the Propagation of the Faith. The Cardinal was overwhelmed by the unexpected honor, but crushed by the cross standing beside it. Rome — Chicago — in juxtaposition! A new life to begin, a transplanting, a second spring! But first: a tearing up by the roots! Once more, and after eighteen years, he was to learn the tortuous lesson of "no lasting city."

At a quarter to six on that March evening the bell rang. Archbishop O'Brien stood at the door. The news was out. "Hello, Juny," said the Cardinal, a hint of weariness in his smile. The Archbishop could not speak. His hand was warm in congratulation; but his lips quivered and he tried very hard to force back the tears. He remained until eight o'clock, summoning all his usual good cheer to the rescue while they talked of the future. He would follow His Eminence to Rome two weeks after his departure. They would spend a month at Como, then return together for the Cardinal's first visit, back to Chicago. Such were Archbishop O'Brien's kindly plans.

It was not long before the wires tingled between Chicago and Memphis. It was good for the Cardinal at this significant moment to hear the warm, southern voice of his intimate friend, Monsignor Merlin Kearny. Their friendship had been long and uninterrupted. Monsignor Kearny had visited the Cardinal frequently both in Milwaukee and Chicago. Sometimes they traveled together and always Msgr. Kearny's lively spirits and ready humor were a source of joy and rejuvenation to the Cardinal.

This time, however, there was no hint of humor in the voice from Tennessee. Monsignor Kearny had counted the cost that this drastic change would put upon his friend. "I do not like the idea of your going to Rome," he said. He was never to forget the Cardinal's unhesitating answer: "It is sweet to be obedient to authority."

Even in those first hours of paralyzing surprise, the Cardinal remembered his flock. He must send them a message, not leave them alone to their speculations. He would explain everything thoroughly and to that end he prepared the following statement:

"When this news came to me, I was surprised and amazed. It never entered my mind that the Holy Father would think of me for such an important office in the Roman Curia, which assists His Holiness in the government of the universal Church. It is clear that His Holiness, in honoring me, principally had in mind honoring the Church in the United States.

"Never before in history has an American prelate been called to such an important office. The Sacred Congregation of the Propagation of the Faith, under the immediate authority of the Holy Father, is entrusted with the care of the foreign missions of the Church. The Catholics of the United States have shown a growing interest in these missions.

"Quite evidently, the Holy Father, in calling me to this office, wished to give another expression of his fatherly appreciation for this interest. At the call of His Holiness I shall go to Rome and with God's help try to prove myself worthy of his confidence and of the great Catholic body of whom I shall be a symbol.

"To my clergy and people on this occasion I express my deep affection. They have been my support and edification through these eighteen years. I know that I shall have their prayers in the discharge of the heavy responsibilities of the office to which I am called. I may say to them that I have not received the official document calling me to this important office.

"When I receive it, I shall inform them in detail on what is involved in this call of the Holy Father. For the present, all that I know is that the Holy Father has called me to be the Pro-Prefect of the Sacred Congregation of the Propagation of the Faith. The Prefect is the esteemed Cardinal Fumasoni-Biondi, whom we remember as being Apostolic Delegate to the United States.

"It will be a great comfort to me to have at my side this great

Cardinal, who, with the exception of his years as Apostolic Delegate in the United States, has been an outstanding official from minor to Prefect of the Sacred Congregation of the Propagation of the Faith. His knowledge of the foreign missions, his great abilities, and his understanding promise me some usefulness in helping the Holy Father in his great apostolate for the missions of Holy Church in these difficult times. May I add that after 18 years here in Chicago, despite my being from other parts, I am a Chicagoan and I love Chicago, its people and its warmth.

"It is my prayer that through the years which God will give me I shall be able to contribute my little part to making Chicago the world's greatest city, in which spiritual values will take precedence over more material and humanistic considerations."

XLIX

WITH even more than his usual energy the Cardinal entered upon the last strenuous weeks of his work as Archbishop of Chicago. He did not cancel any of the engagements that he had made long in advance, and still found time for anything additional that was asked of him. At this time a frequently repeated question was making itself heard with renewed insistence and the Cardinal felt obliged to answer it.

"Why is it that a Roman Catholic cannot become President of the United States?"

"It is very distasteful to me," the Cardinal replied, "to have to answer such an inquiry. As an American citizen who loves his country and its institutions and considers the Constitution of the United States the fundamental law of the world's greatest democracy, I cannot understand why people would ask the question which was proposed to me."

He proceeded to say that since the Constitution forbids any religious test in the election to a civil office, any citizen who meets its requirements may be elected President of the United States. Therefore the fitness of the candidate, not his religion, should be the only consideration. He called attention to the fact that Charles Carroll of Carrollton, a Catholic, was one of the signers of the Declaration of Independence, and that throughout our history the Supreme Court as well as both Houses of Congress included many Catholics.

He declared that the Catholic Church makes patriotism and obedience to civil authority a moral obligation and does not enter the political field. Catholics therefore subscribe without reservation to the Constitution and are in accord with the First Article of the Bill of Rights. "Frankly," the Cardinal concluded, "I cannot understand how any citizen of our country could entertain the thought that a Catholic, because of his religion, is in any way disqualified for any civil office in our country."

On March 24 Cardinal Stritch was with the Benedictines. At St. Procopius' Abbey, Lisle, Illinois, the Benedictine abbot awarded him the Unitas Medal of the abbey, in recognition of his work for Catholic unity.

The Cardinal in accepting the award said: ". . . the modern world needs a concept of the monastic rule of 'pray and work.'. . . The real unity in the Church is the acceptance of the divine origin of the Church, and its test is the acceptance, by all, of St. Peter as the first vicar of Christ." He mentioned also the new post given to him whereby for the first time an American-born cardinal becomes a member of the Vatican Curia, as an expression of this unity in the Church.

It was singularly appropriate that Cardinal Stritch should receive this medal at the conclusion of his regime in America since the past Unionistic Congresses have been held under his patronage. The purpose of this annual congress is to contribute, through discussion, study, and prayer, to the return to the Holy See of dissident Christian groups, especially the Orthodox churches.

Upon the decision that the Cardinal was to remain in Chicago until after Easter, he sent another message to his clergy and to the nearly two million of the faithful belonging to the Chicago Archdiocese. "My heart was heavy," he told them, "with the thought that I must leave you, whom I love with the tenderest fatherly affection. God sometimes in His wisdom asks hard things of us to draw us closer to our Blessed Saviour on the cross. However, in His loving mercy He gives us the graces to say with our Blessed Saviour: 'Not my will but thine be done.' There does come sweet spiritual joy when we do what manifestly is God's will.

"The office to which I have been nominated by the Holy Father carries grave responsibilities and the rarest opportunities to labor with the Holy Father for the spread of the Kingdom of God in mission lands. I would be strangely insensible to noble and exalted motives and indeed wanting in confidence in God, Who gives the graces of office, were I not humbly appreciative of the trust His Holiness has placed in me. As a Cardinal of Holy Church, I would be an unworthy servant if I did not hold the wishes of the Vicar of Christ to be for me a command. Moreover, I would not be true to you if I did not rejoice in the honor which the Holy Father has done you in my poor person. My prayer is that I may correspond with God's graces and prove myself worthy of the confidence which the Holy Father has placed in me, and of your affection, which in these days you so kindly have manifested to me.

"You have been my strength and my joy during the past eighteen years. The accounts of my achievements which are appearing in the press please me, because they are really your achievements. Never has a bishop had a more devoted clergy and laity. This is God's gift to me. Together we have labored and we have labored in no spirit of vainglory, but only for the Church, which is our love and passion. And in the future we shall be united in this same holy spirit and ambition. You have shown your interest in the missions of the Church and have understood that all of us in one way or another must be missionaries. In the office to which I am called I shall have under the Holy Father the missions for my work in Holy Church. We shall be missionaries together. Chicago will be always with me.

"I am not saying 'good-by.' I hope to remain in Chicago until after Easter and to have an opportunity to address you again. This little message is to thank you and to beg your prayers."

We see the Cardinal's feeling for his people in action now. He shares everything with them. They are one with him. If, as he says, never has a bishop had a more devoted clergy and laity, we may also infer that seldom, if ever, has a bishop worked more closely with his people and shown them so well that he loved them. That which we have said concerning his attitude to the Church we now hear more validly expressed in his own avowal: "the Church, which is our love and passion."

He opened his heart also to a number of friends individually. The following excerpts from letters dictated during the six weeks preceding his departure for Rome bring us close to the thoughts and feelings with which he faced the last great challenge of his career. In one of these letters he wrote:

"All through my life I have had only one desire and that is to do whatever God wants me to do. The call of the Holy Father reveals to me God's will."

To an old schoolmate he sends the following lines: "Like you, I have always loved Rome. Rome has been a sort of second home to me. . . . Now I am going back and I shall have residence in Rome. The work will be of course, as you know, very important and will place upon me heavy responsibilities. . . . pray for me through these years and ask God to help me to do His holy will in all things and through my poor person to do lots of good for souls."

Another letter includes the following: "I go not really to a strange place. It may seem queer to some, but I think I know Rome better than any other single city in the world, except perhaps the old part of my native Nashville. . . . When one spends the years between 16 and 22 in a place, he absorbs it. So the fact of going to Rome is not at all a difficulty with me. . . ."

To a friend in Toledo he said: "My mind does go back to the day when I left Toledo. It was with regret and then I had little idea that there would be any more changes in my life. When this news came, I was shocked and surprised, but God has His own ways, and His ways are always the best ways."

A letter to Sr. Inez of the Franciscan Sisters in charge of the Lieutenant Joseph P. Kennedy school at Palos, Illinois, one of the places which the Cardinal specially loved to visit, expresses his deep affection for the Sisters of his household. He wrote: "I know that you and my Franciscan Sisters who are so dear to me and who have been so devoted to me will always pray for me. I remember the day I arrived in the Archbishop's House in Milwaukee. It was all strange. Then there was Sister Fredericka, who at once made me forget what I had left behind. All your Sisters who through the years have been so close to me have been a consolation and a joy. I know that you who are so near to me and who perhaps know me better than any other people in the world are going to pray for me. . . . One thing that pains me is that just at this time I can't take some of my Franciscan Sisters to Rome with me. Maybe in the future, if I have to establish my own home in Rome, I will be writing a letter to the Mother General and begging her to send me some Sisters. I know that my Sisters here in the house will say to the Mother General, 'You must do this for our Cardinal.'"

Another letter contains this pertinent sentence: "If I were to stay here in Chicago and not obey the will of God, I would be afraid for Chicago." The following quotation seems a kind of summary of the closing days of the Cardinal's regime in Chicago: "These days have been very crowded and to get in even the pressing work has taken my time from early morning until after midnight. . . . Always I shall remember that in all my undertakings, humbly and without any selfishness, I have tried to do my best. Perhaps many things could have been done better. Undoubtedly some things have been left undone, because the time was not opportune. I shall do my best and I beg you to pray for me."

The Cardinal did not permit himself to be too busy to travel down to Memphis for the dedication of Maurelian Hall, Christian Brothers College. On March 8 he delivered his last talk in his old home diocese of Nashville. It is impossible to quote it entirely. It is full of charm and reminiscence, with the ever recurring message, like shafts of light, breaking through:

"There is a picture in my memory today. I see the modest, almost shabby guest dining room in the old red-brick Christian Brothers College on Adams Street. At table there were Father Sullivan, etc., etc. . . . and a timid little priest of 23 years, who had finished his studies two months before and been ordained in Rome and had come to Memphis to begin his priestly ministry at old St. Patrick's. . . . May I stop and linger on this memory?" He characterizes several of the old Brothers and says of one of them: "He was jovial, smiling, and very human, and somehow you understood from him that there has to be a smile in genuine piety. The shy little priest said little, but he did see there in these three Brothers what he has come to know so well about the Christian Brothers through many years. . . .

"Today that little priest grown old is here . . . for him all this is like one of those ancient manuscripts on which scholars find the dim imprint of even a more important book, which some scribe before the coming of the printing press erased. . . . The prayers of the Brothers of long ago are being answered, and on the foundations which they laboriously fixed, this college and its future solidly rest." He sees in imagination the old red-brick building shining dimly through the scene of today, like a palimpsest. "Forty-eight years ago I came from Rome to Memphis. In a few weeks I shall go back to Rome. Among the good things God has given me is a close acquaintance with the Christian Brothers which has grown into a friendship. . . . I do not congratulate the Brothers today. That would be idle talk. They look to God for their reward. I do, however, congratulate Memphis. . . . What they have been saying these many years, they say with renewed emphasis today. The advance of science is good. The new inventions are praiseworthy. The new frontiers which are opening before us are inviting. But, unless you keep yourself within the outstretched arms of Christ . . . these things will bring only tragedy and ruin. . . .

"Schoolrooms must not be half playrooms. Basic things must be learned and learned well. . . . A piety which tolerates sloth in the use of the talents God gives, is a sham piety. . . .

"Coming back here today to my own Southland," he concludes, "I thank God that Memphis has these Brothers, and as one who loves Memphis I ask this great city to remember what these Brothers have given it and to see to it that this Christian Brothers College grows and prospers."

Life was stirring in the trees at St. Mary's of the Lake in Mundelein and the early sunlight lay like a promise of spring over the quiet waters on the morning of April 12, 1958. Rows of quiet white figures were kneeling in the sanctuary, the thirty-four seminarians in their long albs, whom the Cardinal was raising to the priesthood. It was his final act as Archbishop of Chicago, and a deep hush rested over the crowded chapel.

The Cardinal looked upon each candidate with love as he administered to him the tremendous powers of the priesthood. Perhaps his own words flashed back into his memory. Perhaps they had remained in his heart throughout the years. Perhaps with the shadow of farewell upon them, he felt them more deeply than ever before: "I would give my right arm if these men remain the kind of priests they are today."

L

IT WAS late one night when the black Cadillac swung toward the northeast corner of North State and made the turn into the driveway leading to the house of the many chimneys. Before it made the turn a lithe figure sprang out of the darkness, apparently from nowhere. The Cardinal was deep in his thoughts until he saw a gun coming through the car window and pointing directly at him. The bandit, however, saw a head with gray hair and recognized it through the shadows. "Gee," he exclaimed, "I didn't know it was you." Before the Cardinal could answer, the would-be holdup fled as quickly as he had appeared.

The Cardinal stirred in his seat, sighed, and walked into the house as calmly as if he were walking upstairs to his study of an evening after dinner. What the thief would have gathered, had he gotten into the Cardinal's pockets, would be an interesting speculation. Had he gotten into the house he might have seen matchbooks lying about, which souvenir collectors vied with each other in acquiring. The Cardinal purposely left them on tables or stands, here and there. They were red, with his coat of arms on one side. The other bore the imprint: "Stolen from Cardinal Stritch."

Whatever the Cardinal's reaction was, from this firsthand experience of attempted assault, we may be certain that he was more concerned about the social conditions in large cities, which made such occurrences more than ever prevalent in late years, and above all the more uneasy about the soul of the bandit, than about any possible danger to himself. It was strange, too, that this should happen at his very door. He had never been molested on his long walks from North Avenue to the uncertain neighborhood of Twelfth Street, nor on his excursions into the ghetto or the Black Belt.

Apparently sputniks and satellites struck no terror into the heart of Cardinal Stritch. "The Sputnik and the Explorer proclaim the order and perfection of law that God placed in nature. Is not the sputnik confounding the very assertion of the communists that there is no God? Why can't they see the truth?"

This declaration constituted part of a sermon that the Cardinal preached on March 11 at Holy Cross Church in Chicago to celebrate the five-hundredth anniversary of the birth of St. Casimir, patron of Lithuania. The Most Rev. Vincent Brizgys, exiled auxiliary bishop of Kaunas in communist-dominated Lithuania, offered the Pontifical Mass at which the Cardinal presided.

This was his first public appearance since the new appointment to which he alluded in a few words: "These days you have been reading many things about me. One thing I shall take with me to Rome — your prayers. I ask you to pray for me. I want to be a good servant of the Church."

Returning to St. Casimir the Cardinal drew attention to the fact that the saint "was living in a day when many Catholics were paying lip service, enjoying luxuries, and when they did not understand that the things given to us on this earth were meant to enrich ourselves spiritually. When we abuse these things, we mar God's work."

St. Casimir's lesson, he said, is "needed today, when new frontiers are being opened by nuclear discoveries and the sending off into space of sputniks and explorers." The Cardinal maintained that the freedom of Lithuania has not been permanently lost. "As we celebrate the fifth centenary of St. Casimir," he said, "the Church and Lithuania are suffering. . . . It makes my heart heavy to know of the suffering of my fellow bishops and priests in Lithuania, of the exile of the people.

"But there is also a note of joy, for the Lithuanians remain the sons of St. Casimir. The spirit of St. Casimir still lives in Lithuania. In these days remember that there is no Easter Sunday unless we climb the hill of Calvary on Good Friday."

During this period of upheaval the Cardinal himself was well on his way up the hill of Calvary. Apart from the emotional strain, the nerve tension associated with the impending parting from Chicago and from America, the speedy winding up of his leading part in the affairs of a tremendous diocese, the global issues of the new position lying in wait, the sudden summons to a change of work, dwelling place, manner of life; apart from all these considerations and the fact of feeling physically unequal to the demands, he had to face the inner pressures of his own thinking. He searched his soul to make sure that neither ambition nor vainglory had the slightest bearing upon his decision, to convince himself beyond the trace of a doubt, that what he was doing was for the best interests of the Church. When the inner answer came and the spirit of obedience brought internal harmony, there was no turning back. When the suggestion came from a good Catholic lawyer: "Eminence, you do not have to go to Rome. According to Canon Law you have the right to refuse," the answer was instantaneous: "There is no case. God has spoken to me by the Pope. There is no case."

On March 17, the apostolic brief formally nominating the Cardinal to his new position having arrived, he had another public statement to make. The text follows:

"I have received the Apostolic Brief by which the Holy Father, Pope Pius XII, has informed me that His Holiness has named me Pro-Prefect of the Sacred Congregation for the Propagation of the Faith in Rome.

"I have arranged to leave Chicago on the 15th of April and to go to Naples on the American Export liner *Independence* from New York on the 17th of April. I shall arrive in Naples on the 25th of April and go at once to Rome by automobile. In Rome I shall be at the Chicago College, Santa Maria del Lago. Immediately on my arrival in Rome I shall take proper steps to assume the duties of my office in the Roman Curia.

"The Sacred Congregations are agencies through which the Pope administers the affairs of the Universal Church. Each sacred congregation has its own clearly defined competence. The Sacred Congregation for the Propagation of the Faith, which in its substantial present structure dates back to the year 1650, has, under the authority of the Holy Father, the care of the missions of the Church. There is a Board of Cardinals, of which, since my creation as a Cardinal in 1946, I have been a member.

"This board meets twice a month under the chairmanship of the Cardinal-Prefect. All important matters, apart from certain routine affairs, are presented to this board, which makes its recommendations, which are presented by the Cardinal-Prefect to the Holy Father for final decision. There is a prelate secretary, presently Archbishop Pietro Sigismondi, who has definite and grave responsibilities. There is a staff of competent officials. The volume of affairs is very large, but the experience of the Church through the centuries has created an organization for the speedy dispatch of these affairs. It is clear that I shall have heavy responsibilities, but it is equally clear that I shall have expert help in the discharge of them.

"Those who have been in Rome will remember the historic headquarters of this congregation in the English-speaking center of Rome, the Piazza di Spagna. This building is one of the artistic treasures of Rome. I shall have my office in this building.

"I know the question which quite understandably the news reporters want to ask me is: What provisions will be made for the Archdiocese of Chicago? Frankly, I must say that in the Church there are decisions which only the Holy Father can make. I would be indeed rash and imprudent if I were to hazard a guess on such decisions. We must leave them to the Holy Father.

"This I do say: that on the 15th of April I shall say 'God bless you' and not 'farewell.'"

That the Cardinal was to have his office in the same building where he once attended classes was a pleasant coincidence. Ever since the early seventeenth century until 1930, when this training college for the missions moved to its new building on the Janiculum Hill, the enormous brownstone edifice, designed by the celebrated architect Bernini, was the home of the College of the Propaganda. The Sacred Congregation then took its place and the classrooms have since been converted into modern offices, a library of reference books on mission work, and lofty galleries housing a collection of decrees and of American, Japanese, Tibetan, Indochinese, African, and South American reference works.

According to the rules of the congregation, the decrees cannot be opened to scholars until they have been on their shelves for a century. Accordingly, decrees handed down in the year 1858 were made available to scholars this year. Another section of the building with a courtyard in the center is devoted to the private apartments of the prefect, Cardinal Fumasoni Biondi, and the secretary of the congregation, Archbishop Sigismondi. Thus one might picture the Cardinal in his Roman surroundings totally different from the unpretentious gray chancery in Chicago.

LI

OFFICE hours at the chancery were proceeding as usual on the morning of March 21 when an unusual visitor appeared and was promptly escorted to the Cardinal's office. His Eminence rose from his desk and with a radiant smile of surprise came forward to welcome Vice-President Nixon. The latter had come to Chicago to speak at the 1958 Nuclear Congress and was eager to profit by the opportunity to tell the Cardinal that his appointment to a high Vatican post was a compliment to the nation. He said that it gives the United States a "recognition it never had before." The Vice-

President remained for about a half hour and said, as he was leaving, that he hoped to visit the Cardinal in Rome the following autumn.

The next paean of praise came to the Cardinal from the floor of the Senate in Washington, where two senators in their addresses congratulated him on the appointment to his new position.

Senator Humphrey of Minnesota described the Cardinal as a "champion of the underprivileged and oppressed," and read to the senators the statement given out by him at the time of the announcement of his designation to the Vatican post. Senator Douglas of Illinois said that the people of his state would miss the Cardinal "very greatly," and expressed gratitude "for his devoted service."

"Catholics and friends of Catholics in the United States and throughout the world," Senator Humphrey said, "rejoiced in the news of his appointment, for the humility and the patience of this brilliant man have earned him the respect and love of all who know him." He said further that although the Cardinal's official title is Archbishop of Chicago, he suspected that "the two titles 'Bishop of the Poor' and 'Bishop of Charity' have more meaning to the people of his see." He recalled what the Cardinal had said long ago: "As long as two pennies are ours, one of them belongs to the poor."

"He has lived that creed," said Senator Humphrey. "Because of his untiring efforts countless hospitals, schools, orphanages, and centers for the mentally ill have been constructed and improved. Cardinal Stritch . . . can look back on a life marked with success in everything he has endeavored to accomplish." He said that the Cardinal is "a liberal, and has fought to see that all people were afforded the chance to integrate themselves religiously, socially, and economically into the life of their community."

Alluding to the fact that most of the mission territories administered by the Sacred Congregation for the Propagation of the Faith are in Africa and Asia, the Senator said: "We all know of the turbulent conditions that exist in those areas, and our hopes and prayers are with him as he takes on these grave new responsibilities."

At this point one begins to wonder whether the Cardinal would subscribe to having himself called a liberal. It is a loose term and can be stretched to fit many a different meaning. One can readily imagine also the Cardinal's aversion to a cliché of any kind. A man may have liberal ideas in some respects and behave like a conservative in others, without wishing to be known either as an out and out liberal or a hidebound conservative. By way of illustration a quotation from Mr. Dann Herr's article, entitled "Prince Among Men," in the January, 1957, issue of *Sign* magazine, may be apt.

"By reputation a conservative," writes Mr. Herr, "Cardinal Stritch has been a friend of labor for many years and has made his archdiocese the American center of new and dynamic apostolic lay groups, some of which still cause nervous twitchings among the more hidebound clerics and laymen. He is famed for his love of people and his delight is being with them, but he is probably the loneliest man in this huge city."

Honors were still being heaped upon the Cardinal. In the latter part of March the Superior-General of the Jesuits sent a document from Rome naming him a founder in the Chicago province of the Society of Jesus, a distinction due to the assistance that the Cardinal gave to the new Loyola Academy. He is the first to receive this honor in the Chicago province which was established in 1928. Every one of the 339 Jesuit priests of the province was pledged to offer three Masses for the Cardinal.

At the end of March he made a final journey to Washington where he was guest of honor at a luncheon at the Apostolic Delegation, with the Apostolic Delegate as host. Ten archbishops and bishops attended, as well as officials of the N.C.W.C. and priests of the Chicago Archdiocese stationed in Washington. The Apostolic Delegate paid tribute to the achievements of Cardinal Stritch and presented the Cardinal with a spiritual bouquet from the staff of the N.C.W.C.

The Catholic Broadcasters likewise had something to give before the Cardinal's departure — an honorary membership in their association. The president, a Claretian Father from San Gabriel,

California, made the presentation. In accepting the courtesy the
Cardinal stressed the importance of work in the field of Catholic
radio and television.

In the meantime the heavy load of work to be done in rapidly
decreasing time did not diminish. Perhaps we can hear the overtones of the fatigue and inner loneliness of these trying days best,
if we listen in on a message from the Cardinal to the man who
continued to be his other self, the secretary of his years in Milwaukee. The latter was away and heard the news over the radio.
Then came the Cardinal's call: "Come back! For your sake and for
my sake! Come back!"

He came. "Romy," said the Cardinal, "I thought this over. It is
the will of God. I wouldn't be a Churchman if I didn't do the will
of the Holy Father."

LII

IT WAS Holy Thursday morning. The Cardinal was to officiate
at the Cathedral, but had not as yet come downstairs. One of the
Sisters, going up to knock at his door, found him in great pain and
unable to get into his cassock. His right arm was giving him trouble
and the perspiration was streaming down his face.

"I have writer's cramp," he said, while the Sister helped him into
his soutane. He would not be deterred, however, from going down
to the Cathedral, although on the way he did admit that his hand
hurt him. With worried faces the priests in the sacristy gathered
about him. "Your Eminence, you cannot say Mass," they insisted.

"O yes," he replied with unruffled calm, "I shall say Mass." He was convinced at last that it would be unwise to attempt the long ceremony of the Mass of the Holy Chrism and permitted the doctor, who had been summoned, to take him home.

It proved to be a muscle spasm. Hot applications gave prompt relief, and the Cardinal lost no time in going back to his work. First, however, he offered the Mass of Holy Thursday in his private chapel for the Sisters, his little daily congregation. For them it was a privilege reminiscent of the past to have him with them for one of the services of Holy Week. From 1943 until the recent change in the liturgy, he had conducted the Tre Ore just for them, on Good Friday. To hear it was sufficient indication that the Passion was one of his favorite devotions. "It was beautiful," said one of the Sisters, "just as though he were meditating out loud."

Beautiful indeed was the daily relationship between the Cardinal and the little community that kept the wheels of home life running so smoothly. "The Sisters know me better than anybody else in the world," he used to say. "If anyone ever writes my biography, they would have to do it." With this recommendation from the Cardinal himself, their testimony may certainly be regarded as firsthand, and it is they who give testimony of his selflessness.

One after the other, with enthusiastic remembrance, each one makes her contribution: "He always thought of others." "He could work all day, typing with two fingers and it was amazing how quickly he could type a talk. 'I won't take any lunch today,' he would say on such occasions." "He could come down to any level. He could talk on any subject. He loved to talk to the bird." "He used to go out and bless the children." "He had something about him that made everyone love him." "He lived close to God." This is both climax and explanation. These are the comments from those, as the Cardinal himself said, who knew him best.

LIII

IN THE little sacristy of the Cardinal's chapel the white vestments were lying in readiness for the morning Mass, when he said: "We must have black vestments today. It is Archbishop Kiley's anniversary and I am offering the Mass for him." The Sister Sacristan looked up with tear-filled eyes. "Yes, Your Eminence," she replied. "Black is more appropriate today."

It was April 15, the day set for the Cardinal's departure. The pain of leaving had been augmented by a call at Mercy Hospital where the Cardinal visited two priests and an old friend. They could not come to him, so he went to them. The old friend, weak and sick as he was, threw his arms around the Cardinal and wept. "Why, oh why?" he repeated. It was almost too much for the Cardinal, especially when, upon leaving the hospital, Sisters, doctors, and nurses had gathered, singing a farewell song as they stood in line to bid him good-by.

The sharpest pain however was yet to be. The most grueling test of the Cardinal's endurance came at midafternoon on Tuesday, April 15, when it was time to leave "the quietest house in Chicago" and to part from the Sisters. The overstrained nerves gave way at last. The Cardinal broke down and wept. "You can't blame me for crying," he said with quivering lips. "I had these Sisters with me for 28 years."

It was over at last. The brokenhearted Sisters found their way to the chapel and the Cadillac with license plate number 1 swung through the driveway and down to the La Salle Street station where the little party was awaited by a throng of perhaps 1500 people.

The Cardinal passed through the crowd, greeting them, pausing as they kissed his ring, on the way to a roped-off area where, over a microphone, he gave them a parting message.

"In leaving you," he said, "I leave with a heavy heart. All I want to say is that I am going to carry you in my heart, and I ask you to carry me in yours. Let us pray that some day you will come to this station to welcome me."

Archbishop O'Brien was beside the Cardinal as he boarded the train, accompanied by a party of thirty, including monsignori, priests, relatives, and some lay friends. Nearly one hundred others followed Bishop Sheil on another train and by plane to New York. Bishop Hillinger and the vicar-general, Monsignor Casey, who had to remain behind to minister to a bereft archdiocese, came to the train, and Mayor Daley represented the city of Chicago in its farewell. As the Twentieth Century Limited steamed out of the station, the Cardinal's words remained as a possession: "I am not saying good-by. This is to thank you and to beg of you your prayers."

LIV

IN NEW YORK on April 16, two Cardinals greeted one another with a warm ecclesiastical embrace. Cardinal Spellman forthwith took Cardinal Stritch to his home on Madison Avenue to be his guest during his short stay in the city. At 12:30 Cardinal Stritch had a conference of a half hour at the Commodore Hotel with members of the press and representatives from radio and television headquarters.

"Now, by a long and devious route, I have become a missionary," he told them. "If you teach Christ Crucified and also teach any man his inherent worth and his dignity as a person, you will make progress in the missions. You always will."

To the American people he said: "If Americans all live our democracy and shoulder its responsibility, we will be a greater force in the world than we could ever be by spending a lot of money." At the close of the interview the Cardinal introduced Archbishop O'Brien, president of the Church Extension Society, as his friend of nearly thirty years.

During the day Bishop Fulton Sheen headed a missionary delegation to greet Cardinal Stritch and to pledge its continued support in his new work. The delegation represented the National Office of the Society for the Propagation of the Faith, of which Bishop Sheen is director. It represented also the Mission Secretariate which in turn represents all the mission societies and all the religious orders and congregations which send out missionaries.

Later in a press interview when Bishop Sheen was asked about his reactions to the appointment of Cardinal Stritch to this position, he replied: "I have many reactions, all of them happy. America has given well over 70 per cent of the aid distributed to the missions every year. It is fitting, therefore, that there be an American cardinal as Pro-Prefect of this Congregation.

"Another reason for rejoicing is that the largest diocese in the United States is now honored. . . . Whereas in Chicago, His Eminence is in charge of only one diocese, now he will be Pro-Prefect of a Congregation which is in charge of 693 dioceses and ecclesiastical jurisdictions."

On the evening before his departure, the American hierarchy honored Cardinal Stritch by gathering for a farewell dinner at the Commodore Hotel. For the last time these four American Cardinals sat together: Cardinal Spellman, the gracious host, Cardinal Mooney from Detroit, Cardinal McIntyre from Los Angeles, and Archbishop Cicognani, the Apostolic Delegate.

In reply to the tributes Cardinal Stritch said: "This is a memory which will linger with me for the rest of my life. It will comfort and console me always. . . . I remember hearing the story of the time when Pope Pius XI had trouble with Mussolini. Someone tried to console him by reminding him that Christ conformed His will to the will of His Father in the Garden of Gethsemane. . . . 'Yes,' said Pius, 'He did conform His will, but first He sweated blood.' So did I in leaving Chicago and all of you. . . . Many things bear heavily on me. I ask your prayers. But tonight I say to you, 'Non addio, ma arrivederci' (Not good-by, but till we meet again)."

LV

CARDINAL STRITCH stood in the bright sunlight on the deck of the liner *Independence* on Thursday, April 17, with the Apostolic Delegate, the three other American Cardinals, and surrounded by a galaxy of prelates and priests who had come to wish him "bon voyage." Cardinal Mooney looked fondly at the friend with whom he had worked so intimately these many years and could scarcely restrain his tears. "Little Brother" he was calling him in his heart, the endearing name with which he had so often addressed him in happier moments.

Cardinal Stritch was calm, smiling in his usual way through this concluding act of the strenuous drama of the past weeks. He had offered his Mass at eight o'clock that morning, at the high altar of St. Patrick's Cathedral and had breakfasted with Cardinal Spellman. Before the steamer slipped from its dock at Pier 84, he sent a final message to his people in Chicago, who, in the words of one of their spokesmen, "couldn't feel worse." He had also a short message for all the people of the United States, reminding them that they have a highly prized gift to give to the world — democracy — and that there are forces in the world with a materialistic philosophy which opposes democracy. "We cannot fight a materialistic philosophy," he said, "with a mere materialistic democracy," and we must muster all our spiritual forces to combat materialism. Before the visitors had to leave the ship at the all-ashore signal everyone on that crowded section of the deck knelt for the Cardinal's blessing. He raised his right arm and pronounced the words of benediction.

LVI

THE ship *Independence* was out on the open sea. The Statue of Liberty had vanished into the western horizon. "She may have her faults; but she's the best there is." The Cardinal had not forgotten that happy characterization. He carried the past with him in his heart as he promised to do. The future lay in God's hands. The present was filled with ready and cheerful obedience. This was sufficient for the moment and the interval of the crossing.

"*Ritorna, ritorna a Roma!*" (Come back, come back to Rome!) the voice of Pius X called from out of the dawn of life. In spirit, the Benjamin that was, had heard and heeded it many times. Was this its last insistent summons? There was indeed "another Pope dressed in white" and as Pius X had promised, it was just the same. A later Pius too was calling: "Come."

This incident of ordination day was in the Cardinal's thoughts now that he was on his way back to Rome. Reminiscently he spoke to his secretary about it. Other words that he had often remembered, and repeated on occasion to American students leaving Rome, were those of Bishop Farrelly describing the incomparable view of the Bay of Naples when seen from the deck of a ship with its prow pointed westward. But the *Independence* had its prow pointed toward the east. They were on the high seas with the Bay of Naples nearing apace. Before they reached it the Cardinal was stricken with intense and unremitting pain in his right arm, and the days that remained were dark with suffering.

During the earlier part of the voyage he had made various observations that throw light upon his feelings. He spoke of what a comfort it was to have his Chicago priests with him at the time of his departure. He alluded also to the consolations which come to the ordinary pastor of a parish, adding that he would gladly trade his position as Pro-Prefect in the Roman Curia to be simply the pastor of a parish. He felt that the higher the position, the more difficult it becomes to remain close to the people. To deal directly with the people was what he really loved.

This attitude is in accord with what he had said a number of years before to his Milwaukee secretary when dressed for a ceremony in his new robes as cardinal "What do you think of the old man?" he had asked playfully. Then he had become serious: "This is so new to me. I had only thought to become a priest."

For hours at a time during this voyage the secretary would sit beside the Cardinal's bed while they talked of Chicago and its priests. How unlike one another many of them were! Even in the seminary they had shown themselves worlds apart, each with his own type of spirituality. "I learned years ago as a young bishop," the Cardinal said, "never to attempt to regiment a rugged spirituality."

Indeed it had never been his way to regiment anyone. He had always respected the individuality of a human being, allowing the branch to grow according to its natural bent, provided always, that the Church was being served thereby. He was not a compromiser, but a conciliator, affable, approachable; perhaps much like Cardinal Hayes had been in his attitude toward charity. During an interview with one of his priests, for example, when an important decision was asked of him, he would listen intently with bowed head and the familiar gesture of pulling at his nose. Then he would come up with the answer "yes"; or if "no," it would be in so gentle a manner that the priest might have walked ten blocks before he knew that the Cardinal had said "no." Though His Eminence was decisive, he was not impetuous. While firmly maintaining his principles, he had the reputation of never offending anyone. This gave evidence of a great fund of patience and an extraordinary gift of understanding. These qualities doubtless played a major part in the valuable contribution he was able to make to the work of the bishops of the United States.

On April 25, with the yellow and white papal flag flying from the mainmast in honor of Cardinal Stritch, the *Independence* docked at Naples. A gathering of ecclesiastics waited at the pier. Archbishop Sigismondi, secretary of the Society for the Propagation of the Faith, was there with Archbishop Castaldo of Naples, Bishop O'Connor, rector of the North American College on the Janiculum, and Monsignor Primeau of Chicago House. Archbishop Pollio of Kaifeng, China, was also present as well as Monsignor Benincasa of the Buffalo Diocese, who was serving in the Secretariate of State; Monsignor Etteldorf of Dubuque, an official of the Sacred Congregation of Oriental Churches, who represented Cardinal Tisserant; and Monsignor Marchi, pastor of the Cardinal's titular church of St. Agnes. In addition there were a number of American priests. Among them: Monsignor Reh of New York; Monsignor Emmenegger of Milwaukee, vice-rector of the North American College; Father Howard, vice-rector of the Chicago House of Studies; Father Cunningham, Paulist, pastor of Santa Susanna, the American church in Rome; and Father Tucek of the N.C.W.C. news service bureau in Rome.

The Cardinal received their greetings, lying in the ship's lounge.

The treatments of the ship doctor had brought no relief. It was plain that the Cardinal was not well. The ring was on his left hand which he extended, while the right arm was tucked inside his coat front. Despite his discomfort he went out of his way to acknowledge the overpowering welcome and even to greet some children who were waiting for him as he left the ship on the arm of a police officer.

In Rome a group of about 200 were waiting at the station to welcome him. Monsignor Tardini of the Vatican was there with Monsignor Brennan of Philadelphia who is a judge of the Roman Rota and an official of the Society for the Propagation of the Faith, besides the representatives of many religious orders. An honor guard of Italian carabineers, the national police, accompanied the Cardinal from the train to his car.

On the very night of his arrival the Vatican doctors consulted as to his condition and on the following day he was hospitalized at the Clinica Sanatrix where he was examined by Dr. Valdoni, cardiovascular specialist. The case was pronounced a thromobotic occlusion of the major artery of the right arm. Two Chicago physicians, Dr. Bergen, the Cardinal's personal physician since he was Archbishop of Milwaukee, and Dr. Keeley of the Loyola Medical School, surgeon of Mercy Hospital and cardiovascular specialist, left Chicago by plane on Saturday, April 26, arriving in Rome on Sunday. Meanwhile the Cardinal's calmness did not leave him. The report on Saturday was that he had passed a tranquil night and that he was in good spirits. The arm was in serious condition, with little feeling in it; but his general condition was good. The doctors were making every effort to avert major surgery and considered it safe to await the arrival of the Chicago physicians before making a final decision. While lying in the hospital the Cardinal said: "Why the fuss? After all, fifty years ago here in Rome in the subdiaconate I gave my body to the Lord. . . . After fifty years, if He wants an arm, I shouldn't begrudge it to Him."

When, after a consultation among the two Italian and the two American doctors, it was declared necessary to amputate the arm as far as slightly over the elbow, the Cardinal received the information with perfect composure. Quietly he awaited the Pope's permission to undergo surgery. This was no longer an imperative procedure; but the Cardinal asked it in a spirit of filial obedience, an act of courtesy toward the Holy Father. The Pope, who had immediately sent his blessing with the hope for a speedy recovery, conveyed the requested permission through one of the secretaries, and the Cardinal accepted the impending surgery with confidence that it was God's will.

In various parts of the world the prayers for him were ascending. A telegram from Vice-President and Mrs. Nixon promised prayers, and the vicar-general of Chicago had requested that special prayers be offered in all the churches of the archdiocese. Throughout the night preceding the operation a major relic of the arm of St. Francis Xavier remained in the Cardinal's room. On the morning of April 28 he received Holy Communion, and all the priests from Chicago House were with him as he awaited the ordeal.

In presence of the two American doctors, of Dr. Rocchi, the personal doctor of Pius XI, and Dr. Galeazzi-Lisi, the Pope's personal physician, Doctor Valdoni performed the operation. In thirty-five minutes it was over. It was not long before the Cardinal revived with extraordinary resilience, the bright smile returned and he could speak to his priests. In the meantime Bishop Atkielski of Milwaukee and Monsignor Hayes, pastor of the Cathedral in Chicago, were flying to Rome and were able to see the Cardinal on the evening after his operation.

"I was surprised," said the Bishop, "to find His Eminence in such excellent spirits and good physical condition. He is a model of courage and spiritual strength." "If I didn't know what happened to you," he said to the Cardinal, "I wouldn't believe it." Before Bishop Atkielski went to the Holy Father for the audience that had been arranged for him, the Cardinal, with his old sense of humor fully restored, said: "Tell him the Archbishop is building churches."

The Holy Father was seated at his desk when Bishop Atkielski was presented. After welcoming the Bishop and asking what America thought of the appointment, the Pope said that he had appointed the Cardinal for his great heart, his great mind, and his facility in Italian; that he will be a great asset to the Church.

LVII

THE Pope at once sent his blessing and congratulations upon the success of the operation with the hope that the Cardinal would soon be able to occupy his new post. Cardinal Fumasoni-Biondi, prefect of the Sacred Congregation for the Propagation of the Faith, was one of the Cardinal's first visitors. Cardinal Micara also came, and a number of other friends in Rome. Cardinal Stritch was anxious to begin his work and expected to leave the hospital during the week end after his operation. The bulletin *Fides*, published by the Congregation, contained the following message: "United prayerfully with the other friends of His Eminence, the members of his new family of the Congregation for the Propagation of the Faith also look forward to greeting him soon, very soon, when he will take up his new work.

The Cardinal was becoming quite active even in his hospital room. From his armchair he presented Dr. Keeley, K.S.G., with the medal and parchment of the decoration which the Pope had given him. He spoke over the transatlantic telephone, and even dictated letters. In his first interview after the operation he said: "Tell the people of Chicago and all over America who prayed for me in my hour of trial, that I am profoundly grateful for the help of their prayers. You don't know how good God can be to you until you have had something like this."

Over the transatlantic telephone from his bedroom in the Sanatrix Clinic his voice rang clear while he said: "I feel fine. I wish the doctors would let me go. But they tell me I must remain here until about the end of next week and rest. I don't want to rest. I want to get out of here and go to my office. There is so much for me to do and I have only one lifetime to do it in — I'm already learning to write with my left hand."

The Cardinal was not in the least sorry for himself. Gently but summarily he brushed aside all expressions of sympathy on the part of his visitors. To the solicitous questioning of one of them he replied with spirit: "Do I feel for the loss of just one limb? No, my son, I thank God He has left me another arm to carry on my work. . . ."

'The first inkling I had of the gravity of my condition," he told an interviewer, "was gleaned from the concerned expressions of the doctors who examined me. I chided them for questioning God's will. If it is His will that I live to carry on the work, then there is nothing to fear.

"If on the other hand it is not His wish, then you are powerless. Let God's will be done. And the surgeon's nimble fingers simplified that will. I live to fulfill God's plan. Strengthened by that knowledge, I am unafraid for the future."

The Cardinal extended a fraternal blessing to Cardinal Spellman of New York, then closed the interview with a blessing and overflowing thanks to the thousands who sent cables and messages of sympathy.

On the second of May the Cardinal walked to the balcony of his room at the Clinic and breathed the outdoor air of spring. How well he remembered the Roman springtimes of student days! For him a new life seemed to open its doors. How new, he was yet to know. It was expected that he would leave the hospital in approximately a week and be able to resume work in about a month. On another lovely day in the sunlit afternoon he was taken for a drive to the

Borghese Gardens. He asked to be driven past St. John Lateran's and looked with love upon the mother church of the world, where he had been ordained. With the joy of recognition he saw the populous streets of Rome again, its campaniles, its somber cypresses, the blue light of the mountains in the distance.

As the days of convalescence went peacefully on, he was permitted to visit Chicago House and even to take his daily luncheon with his priests. It was with the recording equipment there that he dictated two special letters, one of which dated May 7, was directed to Sister Alacoque who was his secretary at home. It reads in part:

"I am now at the Collegio Santa Maria del Lago. They haven't released me from the hospital yet, but they do allow me to go for a ride. I had a fine good lunch today with my own. They have been very good to me at the Clinic and have given me the greatest attention. You would be surprised that in spite of all the pains and suffering, I feel good.

"The doctor told me this morning that the wound is healing and skin is forming all right, and soon I will be able to use that bit of the arm still left me. They cut off the arm between the shoulder and the elbow and they are going to put on an artificial arm. . . .

"I miss you and I miss the Sisters. But you have to make some sacrifices in life. (And don't think that I have been unhappy, don't think that I have been depressed. . . . Somehow or other I have felt that God gave me an opportunity to do something for my people and my priests that I never was able to do.)

"They promise me that I shall be able to do my work. Of course, now I have to regain my strength and I have to get out and do some exercise. Every day I go out in the automobile and when I come here and visit my own, it seems like being back in Chicago. Tell all the Sisters that I thank them for their prayers. (You don't know what the prayers that have been offered for me have done for me. You know it is only when a great trial comes that we really sense being members of the mystical body of Christ. Everything else disappears.)

"So tell the Sisters that I bless them. . . . I have learned, that a right hand is not as important as one thinks it is. Thank God, I have been able to give many blessings with my right hand and I have been able to consecrate bishops and I have been able to ordain many priests. The Holy Father is going to give me permission to say Mass with a priest assistant and that will be a great consolation."

Speaking of ordaining priests, the Cardinal during his convalescence said almost humorously, "When I think of all the times that I said I'd give my right arm! Now He is taking me at my word. . . . I hope that all the priests whom I ordained will remember what I said, and that I've kept my side of the bargain."

The Cardinal's relatives also received a cheerful letter from him, telling of the attention given him, of the mountains of cards and other messages of sympathy that came from all parts of the world, of his eagerness to assume his new duties, of his delight in being able to visit Chicago House. "You would be surprised," he said, "at what I can do with my left arm. God was good to me."

LVIII

"IT IS good to feel like a priest again and return to the altar," the Cardinal said on the morning of May 18, the day set for his Mass in the chapel of Chicago House. It was Sunday. All the priests of Santa Maria del Lago were in the chapel when the Cardinal, assisted by his secretary, Monsignor Hardiman and Monsignor Hayes, pastor of the Cathedral of the Holy Name, went "unto the altar of God." Beautifully, as Monsignor Hardiman testified, His Eminence went through the Mass. In the light of what had been and what was to be, the words of the *Orate Fratres* were aglow with significance: "Pray brethren that my sacrifice and yours may be acceptable to God, the Father Almighty." Then the reply: "May the Lord receive the sacrifice from thy hands to the praise and glory of His name to our benefit and to that of all His Holy Church."

Finally, the *Ite, missa est* — the tremendous assurance that a Mass has been offered, and for the Cardinal a Mass as never before, and never to be again. With what new and understanding fervor he must have said his *Quid retribuam* — "What shall I render to the Lord" and . . . "I will take the chalice of salvation!"

When it was over the Cardinal said with quiet joy: "Well, I feel like a priest again."

As the night of May 18 swung into the early morning hours, the Cardinal was stricken by what the doctors termed a cerebral vascular accident, which left him partially paralyzed and affected his speech. During this last brave battle for life, the world read headlines and waited; for the gentle prelate in his quiet heroism had aroused a sympathy that all but circled the globe. As for the missions, while he could not work for them he was offering his sufferings to help them.

Around the clock, priests and doctors kept their vigil. Monsignor Merlin Kearney, summoned by the Cardinal, and two nephews of the Cardinal, Rev. Morris Stritch from Memphis and Robert Emmet Stritch from Chicago, flew to his bedside. The prosecretary of state, Monsignor Dell'Acqua, came from the Vatican with "an extremely special blessing from the Holy Father in the hope that it might comfort His Eminence." The Pope's blessing is usually sent in writing; but Monsignor Dell'Acqua relayed it orally because, as he said: "In view of the urgency of the case, His Holiness, Pius XII, called me on the telephone at my office at the Vatican and told me to rush here."

Monsignor Dell'Acqua stayed with the patient for ten minutes, then returned to the Vatican to give a firsthand report to the Pope. Before leaving he had said: "His condition appears very grave. However, he understood perfectly that I was giving him a blessing from

His Holiness and seemed very moved. In fact, he was very near to tears."

Toward midnight, Father McCormick, S.J., spent a few minutes in the Cardinal's room. He said that the Cardinal had experienced great spiritual help from the blessing sent by Pope Pius. On May 25, Father McCormick anointed him for the second time since his arrival in Rome.

Sister Nativitas, the night nurse, was already at her post when Signora Bertini, her day duty over, leaned over the Cardinal's bed to kiss his ring as she bade him good night. The light of perfect awareness was in his eyes as he lifted his crucifix for her to kiss. The small crucifix of black wood was constantly in his hand. Gently he would run his fingers over the corpus, and repeatedly he kissed it.

Our Lady, too, was close by, on a post card of the grotto of Lourdes, on his bedside table. They took it away one day, perhaps to make room; but the Cardinal began to show uneasiness as though he missed something until they brought it back. His grateful look told them that this was what he had wanted. All was well now.

Day by day the Holy Father gave proof of his solicitude. Prelates and priests, friends in Rome came to make inquiry. Around the clock his relatives, his priests, his doctors kept their tireless vigil. With deep affection he looked from one to the other. He was perfectly lucid. The keen, quick mind was not darkened while the stricken body fought for life. Throughout it all, there was no sign of struggle in the spirits of the Cardinal. Quietly, as he had done all things, with a smile upon his silent lips, he withdrew into the solitude of his inner self, only the crucifix to bear him company.

Who shall say that in these days of final immolation he was not, more than ever, actually alive? Who shall say that on this lonely promontory the Creator was not permitting his creature to stand revealed, that the world might know Samuel Cardinal Stritch at last, as he was in his essential reality, and be the better for the knowing?

On Wednesday, May 21, the patient showed some signs of rallying. Eventually he was able to formulate a few words: Yes, No, Hello; but as the week wore on the heart began to fail. On Saturday the Cardinal took a turn for the worse and life was plainly at ebb tide. Earlier in the day nevertheless, after he had received Holy Communion as he had done for the past few days, when the attendants asked him whether he was feeling all right, he answered: "Yes."

Beyond the noiseless sickroom, beyond the solicitous ecclesiastical circle, moved the great, spontaneous Roman populace, warm in its sympathy, enthusiastic in its admiration. In this final coming back to Rome, this closing of a career where it had begun, during the short time of his last residence in the Eternal City, the American Cardinal had captured the imagination of the Italian people by the spirit with which he accepted one bitter trial after the other. He had come to live with them. Instead, he was dying among them. From all sides one might hear the exclamation: "*Un Santo, un Santo, è un Santo!*" (A saint, a saint, he is a saint!)

Even after his turn for the worse the Cardinal was still lucid and gave all his attention to the crucifix. In the hopeful days of his convalescence he had even disposed of official business from his sickbed. But now he had other work to do. Now he was placing a new resignation into other hands and those unseen hands were accepting it.

Death was near on Monday the twenty-sixth of May and at noon the Cardinal lapsed into a semicoma, with only moments of consciousness. He did, however, give signs of recognition to his Jesuit confessor, Father McCormick, and at five o'clock in the afternoon he was still conscious. His eyes opened occasionally, and feebly his left hand lifted the crucifix, blessing those around him as he had done in the earlier days of his illness.

The heavy evening hours dropped to midnight. From a window in the Vatican a light was still burning above the square of St. Peter's. The Holy Father, as usual at this hour, was in his study. Almost hourly he had been kept informed of Cardinal Stritch's condition and he knew, as he sat at his desk at midnight, that the spiritual son who had come from afar at his call would receive a further summons at any moment now, and that he would answer the call of Christ with the same ready obedience that he had shown to Christ's Vicar. For him the Eternal City was the short, sure way to Eternity.

The Pope's long day was scarcely over when the watchers at the Cardinal's bedside fell upon their knees and Monsignor Hayes led the rosary and the prayers for the dying. One by one, following Monsignor Hardiman, every priest in the room approached the bed and gave the Cardinal his blessing. Lingering on the verge of eternity he seemed to have been waiting for this; for when the last priest had blessed him, the Cardinal died.

Quietly, serenely, the thronging events of his earthly career had moved toward the peace of this supreme moment of life. As his secretary, Monsignor Hardiman, said later: "All who watched him can never forget. He surely taught us how to die." And the world will agree that the end of the lesson was worth the lifetime of teaching.

While the light of eternity was dawning upon the Cardinal, his priests sank to their knees again and Monsignor Hayes led the prayers for the dead. Once more the intimate procession walked around the bed. One by one every priest kissed the Cardinal's ring, then his forehead. His spiritual sons could not restrain their tears and one of them said: "A holy man has died. There is nothing more to say."

LIX

IN THE North American College on the Janiculum four great candles of unbleached wax burned, steady as sunlight, into the mid-afternoon of May 28. All Rome seemed to have come, not a curious crowd, but a stream of mourners, to pay honor to the American Cardinal who had returned to Rome to die. Only a few days ago, on May 21, it was 48 years since he had become a priest. On that anniversary day he was to have had an audience with the Holy Father. Instead of this a saddened Pope was sending his message of sympathy and blessing to the grieving priests and people of Chicago.

It was nearly a half century since Pius X had said: "*Benjamini miei*" — "My Benjamins, come back, come back to Rome." Oftener perhaps than the others, this youngest of the Benjamins had come back to Rome. On this day St. Pius X resting in his altar tomb between lighted candles in St. Peter's seemed very near to the Benjamin who had loved him; who, on the neighboring Janiculum, was lying uncoffined on a black-draped bier with the candles of Rome about him, clad in the robes of an archbishop vested for Mass. A simple white miter lay just below the gloved left hand. A Crucifix stood at the head, a silver vessel of holy water with a sprinkler at the feet.

All the cardinals came and blessed him, members of the diplomatic corps, prelates, priests, nuns, American friends, and members of Roman families formed a continuous procession. So great was the throng that in a short time the body was removed from the Red

Room, beautiful with its marbles and woods, on the *piano terreno*, as the Italians call the ground floor, to a larger if simpler room with two doors giving onto the wide corridor of the *piano nobile* or first floor.

But Chicago was waiting and Rome had still to give of its best. It was time for the ceremony that was to precede the removal of the Cardinal's body from the North American College to the Jesuit Church of Sant' Ignazio for the Roman Requiem on the following morning. A prelate from the office of the papal master of ceremonies gave a eulogy in Latin, a copy of which was placed in a cylinder at the Cardinal's feet.

After the body was taken from its simple but impressive resting place on a slightly inclined table draped in black velvet, and placed in the coffin of zinc and walnut lined with purple silk which was to carry it to America, Monsignor Primeau, rector of Chicago House, kneeling, placed a scarlet silk veil over the face. In the formal Roman way the casket was closed in presence of the prefect of papal ceremonies, Monsignor Dante, and other officials. Purple ribbon in form of a cross was fastened on the lid with the required official seals marking the death of a cardinal.

Slowly at five-thirty the procession, led by the cross-bearer, moved down the Janiculum. More than 100 seminarians in surplices preceded the glass-walled hearse, with the tasseled red hat resting on top of the coffin. Bishop O'Connor and Archbishop Sigismondi followed, then all the Chicago priests in Rome, the Cardinal's relatives, friends, and 400 priests and seminarians from the North American College, and the College of the Propaganda which included many Asian, African, South American, and Philippine priests.

This universality of representation could only have happened in Rome, and a profound significance inheres in the fact that these natives of the mission countries, to whom the Cardinal was to belong, were at hand to do him honor. The entire combination of circumstances surrounding his final coming to Rome points in some hidden way to what may be called the universality of vocation that was his. In the light of the threefold sacrifice that marked the end of his life, his words assume immortal meaning: "Nearly fifty years ago I dedicated myself to the service of the Church. This is no time to turn back."

In the wake of the universal Church he followed his world-wide vision and with it his intense love for his country constituted a great synthesis of loyalties. When his glowing words and his far-reaching activities could no longer preach, teach, and promote these ideals, he had his sufferings to give. He offered them all for the spiritual benefit of the missions and for his Archdiocese of Chicago. With moving symbolism it happened that on the day following the Cardinal's death, his nephew, Father Morris Stritch, offered a Requiem Mass at the Paulist Church of Santa Susanna, the church for Americans, and on the second day he had his Roman funeral.

Preceded by an escort of motorcycle police, the procession crossed the Tiber into downtown Rome along the Corso Vittorio Emmanuele, then turned left near the Church of the Minerva where the body of St. Catherine of Siena rests, behind the ancient Pantheon, and into the seventeenth-century square fronting the large Church of Sant' Ignazio. The police along the line gave the military salute, some of the women threw kisses as warmhearted Italian women do, military men bowed from the waist and stood at attention. All along the way thousands of Romans, men, women, and children, halted, stopped whatever they were doing and made the sign of the cross conveying the time-honored message: "*Vale in Christo*" (Farewell in Christ).

In the Church of St. Ignatius the body of the Cardinal was placed upon a tremendous catafalque draped in black and gold and surrounded by the traditional one hundred giant, towering tapers. There it rested for the last night in Rome, near the tombs of the youthful Jesuits, St. Aloysius and St. John Berchmans, and the celebrated Cardinal Bellarmine. If the Mass on Thursday was a tribute to Cardinal Stritch on behalf of the universal Church, certainly the throng of more than 2500 persons that poured into the vast, Baroque church of the Jesuits, was its outward manifestation. It included fifteen cardinals of the Roman Curia, the whole diplomatic corps attached to the Holy See, high-ranking prelates of the Vatican and Secretariate of State, visiting prelates, representatives of the Italian government, and the immense congregation, cleric and lay, that fills the churches of Rome on an extraordinary occasion.

Bishop O'Connor celebrated the Mass, with two of the Pope's chamberlains as deacon and subdeacon and the Chicago seminarians assisting at the altar. The Holy Father sent his Sistine choir to sing the Requiem. Many must have been the times that the Cardinal had listened with joy to their superb music and he also had known their celebrated master, Perosi.

During the Mass the Italian guard of honor, the Alpine troops, members of army, navy, and air force, and a military band stood at attention outside of the church. At the elevation of the Host the band sounded the trumpet call, and played Chopin's funeral march at the elevation of the Chalice. The Eternal City gave everything that it could. The cardinals of Rome represented the Catholic world honoring Cardinal Stritch; and Cardinal Tisserant, dean of the Sacred College of Cardinals, administered the final absolution.

For three quiet hours after the Mass the body remained in the church and was then ecorted to Ciampino, the airport where, in presence of an honor guard of Italian troops, it was placed onto a TWA liner for the journey home. While the trumpets were sounding their poignant notes of farewell, the liner lifted its giant wings and swung into the mystery of the sky.

At the Paris airport the Irish ambassador to France came on board to express condolences in the name of the Prime Minister of Ireland. This was the last gracious gesture from the continent of Europe. With its prow turned westward the airship flew through the short spring night, traveling with the dawn as it neared the shore that the Cardinal had left, but little over a month ago.

It was six-forty-five on May 30 when the plane reached New York where it was to stop for two hours before proceeding to Chicago. Bishop Boardman, auxiliary bishop of Brooklyn, with a delegation of priests and laymen, was waiting at the airport. The priests and monsignori who had flown from Rome descended from the plane and joined the waiting group, the fuselage doors opened, and Bishop Boardman blessed the body as it lay on board at Idlewild.

LX

A PALL of quiet lay over Chicago on Friday morning, Memorial Day. Its churches, its city hall were draped in purple and black, its flags floated at half-mast. People by the hundreds were streaming into O'Hare Field, civic and church leaders, representatives of organizations, priests, Sisters, school children. By ten o'clock perhaps 10,000 people from all walks of life were scanning the sky. At ten-fourteen the plane arrived, bringing the dead Shepherd back to his flock.

It was twenty miles from O'Hare Airport to the Cathedral of the Holy Name and for all those twenty miles row upon row of people lined the streets while the slow procession with its motor escort passed. An honor guard of police accompanied the cortege and honor guards were posted at intervals along the way. The following days, from Friday to Tuesday tell a story of love, loyalty, and grief that was new in the annals of the city. Never had Chicago hushed its strident voice to so low and prayerful a pitch. Never had so great a throng moved with such reverent silence. Never had one man so dominated a great metropolis by his gentleness, his charity, his outspoken love for the people.

The cathedral doors were opened wide. Throughout the day and night, from far and near they came, men, women, children, rich and poor, aristocrats and laborers, learned and unlettered, black and white, to look with love and veneration upon the one who had said that he would carry them in his heart. Like the Magi, from different directions the three Cardinals came, Cardinal Mooney from Detroit, Cardinal Spellman from New York, Cardinal McIntyre from Los Angeles. Their thrones were waiting in the sanctuary. Monsignor Benincasa, who accompanied the body of Cardinal Stritch from Italy, was there as the representative of the Vatican and told of the sorrow in Rome over the Cardinal's death. Hundreds of Church dignitaries attended the funeral Mass. Thousands of people were within the church, more thousands were outside, lining the streets for many blocks, willing to stand and watch and wait. Secretary of Labor James P. Mitchell represented President Eisenhower and Archbishop Cicognani, the apostolic delegate, came from Washington to celebrate the Mass.

An impressive pageant, the procession from the rectory to the Cathedral, set out at ten o'clock on Tuesday morning. The Pontifical Requiem Mass began at ten-thirty. Its liturgy was the ritual reserved for a cardinal priest and for royalty. The combined Priests' Choir and the Cardinal's Cathedral Choristers sang the Mass and its magnificent music penetrated beyond the confines of the Cathedral into the listening multitude. The solemn plain chant seemed vibrant with the mourning of the Cardinal's people.

Bishop Cousins of Peoria, now the new archbishop of Milwaukee, preached a sermon that brought the living Cardinal before the congregation, in all his kindliness, in all his graciousness, in all his priestliness. Five absolutions were pronounced over the Cardinal after the Mass was over. When Cardinal Mooney, grief-stricken, uttered the solemn words, it was plain for anyone to see that here was one of the Cardinal's dearest friends.

The last, long procession to Mount Carmel Cemetery and the tireless throng that accompanied the Cardinal to his resting place in Bishop's vault gave further emphasis to the statement that Monsignor Hayes, pastor of the Cathedral, had made: "This is the greatest demonstration of affection for any man, ever witnessed in Chicago."

Volumes could be written about the Cardinal's work, his thought, about his influence upon his times, about his wholeness, his enthusiasm. Perhaps beyond what he could have believed, he fits the very words which he himself once uttered on the subject of enthusiasm. "When God wants to do a thing," he said, "He chooses an enthusiast. He chooses an enthusiast who is well organized, persevering, selfless, and holy."

Bishop Cousins in his sermon expressed the conviction that unborn generations will revere and exalt his name, that of a man whom they never knew. This too corresponds well with a quotation that the Cardinal, in referring to someone else, once added to a personal letter: "Montelambert wrote that only saints and blessed ones have real immortality in this world. They live and work among men from their heavenly home."

With these words in mind it is difficult to think of the Cardinal as lying dead in his tomb at Mount Carmel. He lives, and one cannot help feeling the assurance that he loved men enough to continue working among them from his heavenly home. Bishop Cousins has characterized him also as "a priest of the people, loving them with a deep, Christlike love."

It is on this note of priestliness and his imitation of Christ that this story must end. His likeness to Christ does not call to mind the messianic, kingly concept of the Redeemer which some of the prophets expressed; but rather the Suffering Servant whom the eyes of Isaias saw. He followed Christ the priest, yes; but also Christ the victim, the Agnus Dei, patient at the moment of immolation.

Throughout the Cardinal's story the voice of his Christlike ideal echoes, "this poor old Pope," now St. Pius X: "Come back, come back to Rome!" On the verge of the final going back, the Cardinal said: "Ambition is for young men. I'm going to Rome at the call of Peter." He went to Rome at the call of Peter, to answer in Rome the call of Christ.